ANSWER KE

The Little, Brown Handbook

ELEVENTH EDITION

H. Ramsey Fowler
St. Edward's University

Jane E. Aaron

Longman
New York   Reading, Massachusetts   Menlo Park, California   Harlow, England
Don Mills, Ontario   Sydney   Mexico City   Madrid   Amsterdam

Answer Key to Accompany
Fowler/Aaron: *The Little, Brown Handbook*, Eleventh Edition

1 2 3 4 5 6 7 8 9 10—BIR—12 11 10 09

Longman is an
imprint of

PEARSON

www.pearsonhighered.com

ISBN 10: 0-205-69274-5
ISBN 13: 978-0-205-69274-3

CONTENTS

PART 1

The Writing Process

1 Assessing the Writing Situation

EXERCISE 1.1 Starting a writing journal (p. 3)

Individual response.

EXERCISE 1.2 Analyzing a writing situation (p. 6)

The assignment specifies the subject (the combinations of client, therapist, and theory that tend to make psychotherapy successful), the audience (the instructor and a "discussion group" of classmates), and the purpose (to explain and support a conclusion about the subject). It requires research into studies of psychotherapy. It specifies a length range and a deadline. It does not specify a format, but APA format could be assumed because the course is in psychology.

EXERCISE 1.3 Narrowing subjects (p. 9)

Possible answers

1. How has the availability of video on Web sites such as *YouTube* affected how people form opinions about public figures?
2. How does slang help to bind members of the college community?
3. How does X's theory about math anxiety apply to me?
4. How might term limits affect the House of Representatives?
5. How has immigration affected food choices?

EXERCISE 1.4 Considering your past work: Discovering and limiting a subject (p. 9)

Individual response.

EXERCISE 1.5 Finding and narrowing a subject for your essay (p. 9)

Individual response.

EXERCISE 1.6 Finding purpose in assignments (p. 11)

Possible answers

1. *How has the availability of video on Web sites such as* YouTube *affected how people form opinions about public figures?* Explain how the ability to view video clips of public figures on the Web results in viewers' gaining more information to use in forming their own opinions.

2. *How does slang help to bind members of the college community?* Explain how the community's unique slang contributes to a sense of belonging.
3. *How does X's theory about math anxiety apply to me?* Explain the way X's theory reflects your own experience.
4. *How might term limits affect the House of Representatives?* Argue against term limits for legislators.
5. *How has immigration affected food choices?* Explain how immigrants have vastly increased the variety of foods available. Help readers appreciate this benefit of immigration.

EXERCISE 1.7 Considering your past work: Defining a purpose (p. 11)

Individual response.

EXERCISE 1.8 Defining a purpose for your essay (p. 11)

Individual response.

EXERCISE 1.9 Considering audience (p. 15)

Possible answers

1. *For elementary school students:* physical effects in simple terms; statistics in simple figures; difficulty in quitting once addicted; importance of resisting peer pressure.

   Role: combined teacher and parent. Tone: warm, slightly admonitory.

   For adult smokers: graphic depiction of physical effects; detailed statistics; influence on children; effect on smoker's appearance, odor, breath.

   Role: combined friend and lecturer. Tone: no-nonsense.

2. *For cyclists who oppose the law*: status of law; reasons for opposition; need for action; suggested actions.

   Role: peer, motivator. Tone: informal, urgent.

   For people who favor the law: acknowledgement of pro-law position; disadvantages of helmets; lack of proven need; infringement of cyclists' rights.

   Role: Fellow citizen. Tone: informative, reasonable, appealing to shared values.

3. *For your neighbors:* feelings of neighborhood residents; dangers to children and pets; lowered property values; threat of petition to zoning board.

   Role: peer. Tone: direct, a bit angry.

   For the zoning board: violation of zoning regulations; length of time the wrecked truck has been present; number of unsuccessful appeals to neighbors; dangers to children and pets.

   Role: plaintiff. Tone: serious, reasonable.

EXERCISE 1.10 Considering your past work: Writing for a specific audience (p. 15)

Individual response.

EXERCISE 1.11 Analyzing the audience for your essay (p. 15)

Individual response.

2 Developing and Shaping Ideas

EXERCISE 2.1 Considering your past work: Developing a topic (p. 26)

Individual response.

EXERCISE 2.2 Keeping a journal (p. 26)

Individual response.

EXERCISE 2.3 Using freewriting, brainstorming, or clustering (p. 26)

Individual response.

EXERCISE 2.4 Sending an online query (p. 27)

Individual response.

EXERCISE 2.5 Developing your subject (p. 27)

Individual response.

EXERCISE 2.6 Evaluating thesis statements (p. 32)

1. The statement lacks unity because the two halves do not seem to relate to each other.

   Possible revision: We should channel our natural feelings of aggression toward constructive rather than destructive ends.

2. The statement needs to be more specific and significant: How is Islam misunderstood? So what?

   Possible revision: Americans' misconceptions about Islam—especially that it is fanatical and oppressive—contribute to global instability.

3. The statement needs to be more specific: How do manners work as "social glue"?

   Possible revision: Manners are a kind of social glue, binding people together by regulating the interactions of acquaintances and strangers alike.

4. Good thesis statement: significant, specific, and unified.

5. The sentence simply states a fact.

   Possible revision: The poem depicts motherhood as a saintly calling.

EXERCISE 2.7 Considering your past work: Developing a thesis (p. 32)

Individual response.

EXERCISE 2.8 Drafting and revising your own thesis statement (p. 32)

Individual response.

EXERCISES 2.9 and 2.10 Organizing ideas and **Creating a formal outline** (pp. 44–45)

Possible answer

I. In the past, professional soccer tried but could not get a foothold in the United States because of poor TV coverage and lack of financial backing.
   A. Professional soccer tried but could not get a foothold in the United States. [new general idea]
      1. Isolated events such as the US's hosting of the World Cup in 1994 greatly increased American interest in soccer.
      2. Past American interest in soccer quickly died down.
   B. In the United States the success of a sport depends largely on its ability to attract huge TV audiences.
      1. Soccer was not often presented on US television.
      2. Potential fans did not have a chance to see soccer games.
   C. Failures like that of the start-up North American Soccer League made potential backers wary of new ventures.

II. Recently, the outlook for professional soccer has changed dramatically.
   A. Professional soccer has attracted both TV audiences and financial backing. [new general idea]
      1. The US television audience for soccer's 2007 World Cup final was larger than the average US television audience for baseball's World Series the same year.
      2. Investors have poured hundreds of millions of dollars into Major League Soccer, the US professional league.
      3. Many of Major League Soccer's games are well attended, and some of its teams are making a profit.
   B. The growing Hispanic population in the United States could help soccer grow as well.
      1. In countries of South and Latin America, soccer is the favorite sport.
      2. In 2007, soccer's World Cup final was broadcast on ABC and on Spanish-language Univision.

EXERCISE 2.11 Considering your past work: Organizing ideas (p. 45)

Individual response.

EXERCISE 2.12 Organizing your own essay (p. 45)

Individual response.

3 Drafting and Revising

EXERCISE 3.1 Analyzing a first draft (p. 50)

Possible answers

Some significant differences between Moreno's scratch outline and her first draft:

- Moreno gives a detailed summary of Friedman's essay in paragraphs 1 and 2.
- In paragraph 3, Moreno gives work experience and education as evidence of her mother's excellent technical skills.
- In paragraph 5, Moreno explains the kinds of classes she plans to take to obtain a well-rounded education.
- In the conclusion, Moreno addresses a new topic, hard work, which was not part of her scratch outline.

EXERCISE 3.2 Considering your past work: Drafting (p. 50)

Individual response.

EXERCISE 3.3 Drafting your essay (p. 50)

Individual response.

EXERCISE 3.4 Analyzing a revised draft (p. 59)

Individual response.

EXERCISE 3.5 Considering your past work: Revising (p. 59)

Individual response.

EXERCISE 3.6 Revising your own draft (p. 59)

Individual response.

EXERCISE 3.7 Considering your past work: Editing (p. 65)

Individual response.

EXERCISE 3.8 Editing your own draft (p. 65)

Individual response.

EXERCISE 3.9 Proofreading (p. 68)

An environmental group, Natural Resources Defense Council, has estimated that 5,500 to 6,200 children who are in preschool today may contract cancer during their lives because of the pesticides they consume in their food. In addition, these children will be at greater risk for kidney damage, problems with immunity, and other serious impairments. The government bases its pesticide-safety standards on adults, but children consume many more of the fruits and fruit products likely to contain pesticides.

EXERCISE 3.10 Preparing your final draft (p. 68)

Individual response.

4 Writing and Revising Paragraphs

EXERCISE 4.1 Finding the central idea (p. 77)

1. The central idea is sentence 8: The black bourgeoisie feel a sense of shame about their own identity.
2. The central idea is sentence 1: Scientists know something about the song of the humpback whale.

EXERCISE 4.2 Revising a paragraph for unity (p. 78)

The topic sentence is sentence 1. Unrelated are sentences 4 and 7.

EXERCISE 4.3 Considering your past work: Paragraph unity (p. 78)

Individual response.

EXERCISE 4.4 Writing a unified paragraph (p. 79)

Delete statements not pertaining to Mozart's accomplishments: when he was born, where he lived, when he married, his debts. Possible paragraph:

> Mozart's accomplishments in music seem remarkable even today. At the age of six he made his first concert tour of Europe, playing harpsichord, organ, and violin. He had begun composing music at the age of five, and by adolescence he had published numerous musical compositions. When he died at thirty-five, his work included over six hundred compositions, most notably operas, symphonies, quartets, and piano concertos.

EXERCISE 4.5 Turning topic sentences into unified paragraphs (p. 79)

Individual response.

EXERCISE 4.6 Analyzing paragraphs for coherence (p. 90)

1. Lieber paragraph (p. 78): Organization: general to specific. Parallelism after first sentence: *They have measured . . . recorded and studied . . . learned*. Repetition: *whale, sings, song*. Pronoun: *they*. Transitional expression: *And.*
2. Begas paragraph (p. 93): Organization: chronological. Parallelism: *They persuaded . . . they deprived; Jill became . . . she dropped out*. Repetition: *lonely, college/school*. Pronouns: *Jill/she; men and women/they*. Transitional expressions: *Between . . . , increasingly, Before long, too.*
3. Dyson paragraph (p. 95): Organization: climactic. Parallelism and repetition: *reason is the need . . . reason is the need . . . reason is our spiritual need*. Further repetition: *space, earth/this planet*. Pronouns: *we, our, us*. Transitional expressions: *first, second, third*.

EXERCISE 4.7 Arranging sentences coherently (p. 90)

The coherent order would be 1, 2, 5, 3, 6, 4

EXERCISE 4.8 Eliminating inconsistencies (p. 90)

The Hopi tihu, or kachina likeness, is often called a "doll," but its owner, usually a girl or woman, does not regard it as a plaything. Instead, she treats it as a valued possession and hangs it out of the way on a wall. For its owner the tihu represents a connection with the kachina's spirit. It is considered part of the kachina, carrying a portion of the kachina's power.

EXERCISE 4.9 Using transitional expressions (p. 91)

Possible answers

1. *Yet, However, Even so,* or *Nevertheless*
2. *even, also,* or *further*
3. *As a result, Consequently,* or *Therefore*

EXERCISE 4.10 Considering your past work: Paragraph coherence (p. 91)

Individual response.

EXERCISE 4.11 Writing a coherent paragraph (p. 91)

Possible paragraph

Hypnosis is far superior to drugs for relieving tension. It is inexpensive even for people who have not mastered self-hypnosis, whereas drugs are expensive. It is nonaddictive, whereas drugs foster addiction. And most important, hypnosis has none of the dangerous side effects of drugs, such as weight loss or gain, illness, and even death.

EXERCISE 4.12 Turning topic sentences into coherent paragraphs (p. 92)

Individual response.

EXERCISE 4.13 Analyzing paragraph development (p. 102)

1. Gates paragraph (p. 78): Patterns of development: cause-and-effect analysis and illustration. Supporting information: mainly the example in sentences 4–8.
2. Wax paragraph (p. 83): Pattern of development: cause-and-effect analysis. Supporting information: first three sentences.

EXERCISE 4.14 Analyzing and revising skimpy paragraphs (p. 102)

Possible answers

1. Sentence 1 requires some expansion to explain *quality of communication*. Each of the next two sentences needs to be supported with specific examples of the two qualities named.
2. Sentences 2, 3, and 4 should each be followed by at least two specific examples of gestures to make the writer's meaning concrete.
3. Sentences 2 and especially 3 require specific support: examples of easy changes, advantages of trying out different versions, and clarification of *the hard work of revising*. What does it involve? Why is it *hard?* Why is it different from what a word processor can do?

EXERCISE 4.15 Considering your past work: Paragraph development (p. 102)
Individual response.

EXERCISE 4.16 Writing with the patterns of development (p. 103)
Individual response

EXERCISE 4.17 Analyzing an introduction and conclusion (p. 110)
Possible answer

The introduction in the first draft rushes to a short summary of Friedman's essay without first securing the reader's interest, and it moves to the thesis statement without carefully connecting the essay to the thesis. In contrast, the final introduction opens with an engaging question and a provocative answer that leads smoothly into Moreno's thesis.

The conclusion in the first draft goes in a new direction by introducing the importance of working hard in college, which is not addressed elsewhere in the essay. In the final draft, the conclusion restates Moreno's points of agreement and disagreement with Friedman (her thesis) and finishes by looking toward the future.

EXERCISE 4.18 Considering your past work: Introductions and conclusions (p. 110)
Individual response.

EXERCISE 4.19 Analyzing paragraphs in an essay (p. 112)

Possible answer

Throughout the essay, Moreno repeats or restates key terms: *outsourcing, globalization; education, academic experience; communication, communicate, writing, communicators; technical training, technical expertise, technical skills; problem solver, proposing solutions*. For each main point, the opening sentence connects specifically to the thesis statement. The pronouns *I/me, she/her,* and *they/their* appear consistently. Transitional expressions (*At first glance, however, First, Still, Also,* and many others) link sentences and paragraphs. (Further analysis of this essay appears in Chapter 3 of the handbook and in the answer to Exercise 4.17.)

EXERCISE 4.20 Considering your past work: Paragraphs in the essay (p. 112)
Individual response.

5 Designing Documents

Exercise 5.1 Redesigning a paper (p. 121)
Individual response.

PART 2

Reading and Writing in College

6 Developing Academic Skills

Chapter 6 does not have any exercises.

7 Forming a Critical Perspective

EXERCISE 7.1 Reading (p. 141)

Individual response.

EXERCISE 7.2 Summarizing (p. 146)

Possible answer

As their support of the government's student loan program illustrates, politicians ignore the economic reality that using resources to benefit one group (students in debt) involves taking the resources from another group (taxpayers). Students' average debt is not even that high, and college graduates can afford to pay it off. The greatest attention is paid to the graduate with a large debt, but the law also allows affluent students to borrow, even if their parents profit and the students drop out of school or waste time there. Funded by taxpayers, the loan program has contributed to declining educational standards, rising tuitions, and rising professors' salaries. Taxpayers should balk at funding the program further.

EXERCISE 7.3 Thinking critically (p. 152)

Possible answers

1. *Analysis:* What is the basis for the author's comparison of print and televised journalism? The key words are *demand reading, not just viewing.*

   Interpretation: Are better . . . than implies a value judgment. *Demand reading, not just viewing* reveals the author's assumption that viewing is somehow less worthy than reading, perhaps because viewing is more passive.

   Synthesis: This author prefers print journalism and disparages television journalism because of the different activities needed to partake of them.

Evaluation: This statement shows the author's bias in favor of written news and implies some contempt for TV news. The author's reasons for preferring reading over viewing are not evident and require explanation. Some other questions: Are people who get their news from TV less well informed than those who get it from reading? Even if television news is inferior, isn't it better than no news at all (for those who won't or can't read)? Might television news be preferable for its immediacy?

2. *Analysis:* What is the author's purpose? The key words are *true, democratic, giving voice to,* and *people of all persuasions.*

   Interpretation: Democratic means "of or for the people." *True democratic forum* means that there are competing, perhaps misleading, forums. *Giving voice to people* appeals to a sense of fair play and belief in free speech, while *all persuasions* implies open-mindedness. The author assumes that people need a public forum where they can voice their opinions. Because it is immediate, radio gives people the freedom to say what they want. Other forums may censor or restrict who can say what.

   Synthesis: The writer values radio call-in shows for affording all kinds of people a chance to express themselves without censorship.

   Evaluation: This writer evidently believes that radio is somehow freer than other places for people to speak their minds. What other forums for free speech are there? Does radio censor or alter the opinions expressed? (What about the time delays for excluding objectionable language?) Are "people of all persuasions" really calling such shows, or just some kinds of people? Are unedited, inexpert opinions a democratic necessity?

3. *Analysis:* What is the author's attitude toward participation in online communities? The key words are *threaten, undermine, ability,* and *interact face to face.*

   Interpretation: Threaten and *undermine* imply danger; *ability* and *interact face to face* imply that face-to-face communication is a kind of skill or talent. Together the words imply that the skill or talent is vulnerable, subject to some kind of destruction. The author's assumptions: Online and face-to-face interaction are different. Face-to-face interaction has an intrinsic value. Online interaction does not have this value. Interacting online diminishes this value.

   Synthesis: The author believes that something valuable will be lost to online interaction.

   Evaluation: This statement indicates a preference for face-to-face interaction over online interaction and a concern about the latter's overwhelming the former. But what exactly is special about face-to-face interaction? What does it provide that participation in online communities doesn't? Won't people continue to meet face to face even if they also interact online? Will online communities necessarily undermine face-to-face interaction? Might online communities also contribute something positive of their own, adding to rather than subtracting from the ways people interact?

EXERCISE 7.4 Reading an essay critically (p. 153)
Individual response.

EXERCISE 7.5 Reading a magazine critically (p. 153)
Individual response.

EXERCISE 7.6 Viewing an image critically (p. 161)
Individual response.

EXERCISE 7.7 Viewing an image critically (p. 161)
Individual response.

EXERCISE 7.8 Comparing images critically (p. 161)
Individual response.

8 Writing in Academic Situations

EXERCISE 8.1 Using academic language (p. 170)
Possible revision

The stereotype that women talk more on cell phones than men do turns out to be false. In a five-year study of 1021 cell phone owners, a major wireless company found that men spend 35 percent more time on their phones, talking an average of 571 minutes a month compared to the women's average of 424 minutes a month. Women do talk more on home phones than men do, but that difference is declining.

EXERCISE 8.2 Considering your past work: Writing in academic situations (p. 170)
Individual response.

EXERCISE 8.3 Considering your native language or dialect (p. 170)
Individual response.

EXERCISE 8.4 Responding to critiques (p. 176)
Individual response.

EXERCISE 8.5 Writing critically about a text (p. 176)
Individual response.

EXERCISE 8.6 Writing critically about an image (p. 176)
Individual response.

EXERCISE 8.7 Writing critically about an image (p. 176)

Individual response.

EXERCISE 8.8 Writing critically about several images (p. 176)

Individual response.

9 Reading Arguments Critically

EXERCISE 9.1 Reading arguments critically (p. 187)

Possible answers

Kirkpatrick Sale essay

Claims: Thesis (paragraph 5): Individuals' conservation efforts do not raise the consciousness necessary to solve the ecological crisis. Supporting claims: Individuals' conservation does not make a significant dent in energy consumption dominated by industry and government (1, 2). The ecological crisis requires a *drastic overhaul of this civilization,* not individual *life-style solutions* (3). Such solutions divert individuals from *the hard truths and hard choices* of truly changing consciousness (4).

Evidence: Statistics and other facts: 2–5. Examples: 1, 3–5. Appeals to beliefs or needs: mainly, we should do what's necessary to solve the ecological crisis (throughout).

Assumptions: Notably: There is an environmental crisis. It must be solved. Ozone depletion and rain forest destruction are *corporate crimes* (2). Industry and government are powerful and self-protective. They will not respond appropriately to the ecological crisis unless forced to do so by the people. The people are unwilling to make more than life-style changes to solve the crisis.

Tone: No-nonsense (*I don't . . . believe that I am saving the planet*), unrestrained (*patently corporate crimes; truly pernicious*), sardonic (*"all of us"; "our" control; life-style solutions; write-your-congressperson solutions*).

Reasonableness: Sale is obviously biased, so his reasonableness will probably reside in the eye of the beholder. He does offer evidence for his key assertion about the environmental responsibility of industry and government, and his examples show him to be familiar with the mentality of most recyclers (a group he even includes himself in). He acknowledges the opposition most clearly in paragraph 5, where he rebuts the claim that the individualistic approach is at least a start on consciousness raising.

Fallacies: See the answer to Exercise 9.4.

Evaluation: Answers will vary.

Oil corporation advertisement

Claims: Thesis (paragraphs 2, 6, 10, 13): Myths about oil exploration, waste, and conservation do not address America's true energy needs. Supporting claims: Offshore drilling is necessary and does not unduly pollute

(4). Though heavy, America's energy use is appropriate for the nation's size and productivity (7, 9). Favoring conservation over exploration would increase oil imports or stop economic growth (12).

Evidence: Statistics and other facts: 3–4, 7–9, 12. Examples: 3. Appeals to beliefs or needs: Mainly, America is a strong country whose economic health is crucial for all (throughout).

Assumptions: Notably: Policy needs to be guided by truths, not myths. Importing foreign oil is undesirable. Some pollution is inevitable and acceptable. America is justified in using energy proportionate to its size and productivity. Conservation is desirable. Economic growth is essential.

Tone: Sincere (*a mystery we hope puzzles others as much as it does us; We probably can—and should—do more*), candid (*Truth is; The fact is; In fact; Let's face it; No doubt about it*), perplexed (*We always have such a problem; where is the waste*).

Reasonableness: Like Sale's essay, the ad is strongly biased, but the statistics and other facts and the sincere tone contribute to a sense of reasonableness. So do the several bows to the opposition, including the statements of the objectionable myths themselves and the support for conservation.

Fallacies: See the answer to Exercise 9.4.

Evaluation: Answers will vary.

EXERCISE 9.2 Analyzing advertisements (p. 195)

Individual response.

EXERCISE 9.3 Identifying and revising fallacies (p. 195)

Possible answers

1. Begged question, argument ad populum, and false analogy.

   A revision: The fact that individuals in the United States cannot legally sell nuclear technology to nonnuclear nations, while the government can, points up a disturbing limit on individual rights.

2. Sweeping generalization and begged question.

   A revision: A successful marriage demands a degree of maturity.

3. Hasty generalization and non sequitur.

   A revision: Students' persistent complaints about the unfairness of the grading system should be investigated.

4. Either/or fallacy and hasty generalization.

   A revision: People watch television for many reasons, but some watch because they are too lazy to talk or read or because they want mindless escape from their lives.

5. Reductive fallacy and begged question.

   A revision: Racial tension may occur when people with different backgrounds live side by side.

EXERCISE 9.4 Identifying fallacies in arguments (p. 196)

Possible answers

Though free of the most egregious appeals, the Sale essay and the advertisement both demonstrate several basic fallacies. Most notably:

Kirkpatrick Sale essay

Either/or: Either we achieve a *drastic overhaul of our civilization* or the environment will be destroyed (paragraph 3).

Begged question: The individualistic approach to environmental problems does not *challenge the belief in technofix or write-your-Congressperson solutions* [Do these not work?] or achieve an essential, fundamental change in thinking [Is the change essential?] (5).

False analogy: The analogy between recycling centers and hospitals (5) implies that a preventive approach (*ecological criteria* for packaging and production; preventive medicine) would eliminate the need for the institution. This isn't true of hospitals (people would still get sick), so how is it true of recycling centers?

Oil corporation advertisement

Begged question: The fact is, oil industry offshore drilling operations cause less pollution than other sources of pollution (4). [But how much pollution do the drilling operations cause?]

Either/or: Either we move everyone to one place or we continue to use a disproportionate amount of the world's energy (7).

Either/or: Either we find more energy or the economy will not grow; either we find more energy or we will have to increase imports (2).

Begged question: Despite good conservation efforts, we still need petroleum exploration (12). [But why can't conservation be improved to eliminate the need for risky exploration?]

EXERCISE 9.5 Identifying fallacies online (p. 196)

Individual response.

10 Writing an Argument

EXERCISE 10.1 Finding a subject for argument (p. 197)

Possible answers

Topics that are not appropriate for argument:

2. A matter of facts, and few people would disagree.
4. A matter of facts, and few people would disagree.
8. A matter of personal preference.
9. A matter of facts.
10. A matter of personal belief.

EXERCISE 10.2 Conceiving a thesis statement (p. 198)
Possible answers

Thesis statements for appropriate topics in Exercise 10.1:

1. An athletic scholarship should be what the term implies: an award to one who is both a superior athlete and a superior scholar.
3. Although censoring the Web sites of hate groups might offer some protection to persecuted groups or individuals, such censorship would be far too costly to free speech.
5. Until the city can construct private housing for the homeless, it must do more to make public shelters safe and clean.
6. Billboards help to destabilize urban neighborhoods by creating the impression that the neighborhoods are mere roadways.
7. Humane testing methods are adequate enough that cosmetics companies do not have to abuse animals in testing.

EXERCISE 10.3 Analyzing purpose and audience (p. 199)
Individual response.

EXERCISE 10.4 Reasoning inductively (p. 203)

The unreasonable generalizations from the given evidence are statements 2 (can't be inferred from the facts), 3 (contradicted by the facts), and 5 (can't be inferred from the facts).

EXERCISE 10.5 Reasoning deductively (p. 203)

Possible answers

1. *Premise:* Anyone who has opposed pollution controls may continue to do so.
   Premise: The mayor has opposed pollution controls.
   Conclusion: The mayor may continue to do so.
   The statement is valid and true.

2. *Premise:* Corporate Web sites are sponsored by for-profit entities.
   Premise: Information from for-profit entities is unreliable.
   Conclusion: Information on corporate Web sites is unreliable.
   The statement is untrue because the second premise is untrue.

3. *Premise:* Many good artists trained at Parsons.
   Premise: Schroeder trained at Parsons.
   Conclusion: Schroeder is a good artist.
   The statement is invalid because the first premise does not necessarily apply to the second.

4. *Premise:* Those who use their resources to help others deserve our particular appreciation.
   Premise: Some wealthy athletes use their resources to help others.
   Conclusion: Some wealthy athletes deserve our particular appreciation.
   The statement is valid and, if the first premise is accepted, true.

5. *Premise:* Any employer who has hired only one woman is sexist.
   Premise: Jimson is an employer who has hired only one woman.
   Conclusion: Jimson is sexist.
   The statement is untrue because the first premise is not true: there may be other reasons besides sexism for hiring only one woman.

EXERCISE 10.6 Using reason and evidence in your argument (p. 205)

Individual response.

EXERCISE 10.7 Identifying appeals (p. 208)

Possible answers

1. Primarily emotional appeal. Ethical appeal: knowledgeable, concerned, reasonable (at least in the two uses of *may*), slightly sarcastic (*most essential of skills*).
2. Primarily rational appeal. Ethical appeal: knowledgeable, reasonable.
3. Primarily rational appeal. Ethical appeal: knowledgeable, fair, willing to acknowledge opposing views.
4. Primarily emotional appeal. Ethical appeal: sympathetic toward animals (but perhaps unfair to *so-called scientists*).
5. Primarily rational appeal. Ethical appeal: knowledgeable, fair, willing to acknowledge opposing views.

EXERCISE 10.8 Reaching your readers (p. 209)

Individual response.

EXERCISE 10.9 Organizing your argument (p. 210)

Individual response.

EXERCISE 10.10 Writing and revising your argument (p. 211)

Individual response.

EXERCISE 10.11 Critically reading an argument (p. 215)

1. *Claims* related to the thesis statement: the last sentences of paragraphs 3, 5, and 7; the first and last sentences of paragraph 8; and the conclusion. *Evidence*: studies cited in paragraphs 2, 3, 4, 5, 7, and 9; evidence gathered by the author in paragraphs 4 (comedy programming) and 6 (educational programming).
2. *Appeals to reason:* mainly, the use of studies as evidence (pars. 2, 3, 4 5, 7), the tempered claim (pars. 8, 9), and the deductive argument (replacement voices can be helpful; television provides replacement voices; therefore, television can be helpful). *Appeals to emotion:* sympathy for the lonely (par. 2), appreciation of children (par. 6). The argument is mainly rational.
3. The ethical appeal is that of a fair-minded, reasonable person.
4. *Appeals made by the illustrations:* Responses about the effectiveness of the illustrations will vary. Some of the appeals:

Fig. 1 backs up the claim that TV can ease loneliness (rational appeal), shows the man enjoying himself (emotional appeal), and conveys the writer's competence in choosing an appropriate image (ethical appeal).

Fig. 2 strengthens the claim that laughter is healthful with information from a reliable source (rational appeal), arouses curiosity with an unusual combination of photograph and diagram (emotional appeal), and proves the writer trustworthy and fair with the caption's acknowledgement that the source does not merit TV watching (ethical appeal).

Fig. 3 supports the claim that TV can educate children by showing children with a character from a respected educational program (rational appeal), depicts a familiar, comfortable character and cute, smiling children (emotional appeal), and shows sensitivity to readers' probable knowledge as well as seriousness.

5. The objections are raised and answered in paragraph 8: too much TV is harmful, and replacement voices are not enough. Both objections are accepted as valid.
6. Individual response.
7. Individual response.

11 Reading and Using Visual Arguments

EXERCISE 11.1 Reading a visual argument critically (p. 222)

Possible answers

1. The audience seems to be people who are serving or might serve as Big Brothers or Big Sisters (primarily the latter since the people depicted are female). The happiness and togetherness of the subjects would reinforce the commitment of current volunteers and invite the participation of others.
2. The organization fosters pairings of adults and children and emphasizes togetherness and having fun.
3. The main claim is in the large text: "Time spent with you is like a day on the beach." In other words, the relationship of volunteer and child is carefree, invigorating, and fun.
4. The photograph provides the evidence for the claim: the beach is inviting, the subjects are happy, lively, and affectionate.
5. Some assumptions: Happy, affectionate relationships are good for adults and children. The smiling subjects are in fact a volunteer and her "little sister." A day at the beach is an appealing prospect and a desirable parallel for a relationship.
6. The most noticeable elements of the image are the subjects' feet, the subjects' smiles and windblown hair, and the bright background, all conveying beach fun. The foregrounded bare feet, especially, empha-

size freedom and playfulness. The large type across the woman's feet further focuses attention on them.

7. Individual response.

EXERCISE 11.2 Identifying fallacies in visual arguments (p. 222)

Individual response.

EXERCISE 11.3 Brainstorming images for a visual argument (p. 226)

Possible answers

1. Images helpful: photographs of seniors and their pets; graph relating pet care and life improvement.
2. Images somewhat helpful: photographs of people gathered in building entrances or other places were smokers congregate; emphasizing variety of people and obvious interactions.
3. Images essential: Military recruitment ads targeted to certain kinds of people.
4. Images helpful: photograph of solid-waste landfill; chart showing current and proposed volume of campus waste; diagram showing proposed recycling process.
5. Images not helpful unless data demonstrate a relationship between music listening and information retention.

EXERCISE 11.4 Filling gaps in a visual argument (p 227)

Additional images might include a graph showing the correlation between the number of children and adolescents who view movies in which stars smoke and the number of children and adolescents who start smoking, or a graph showing the average number of instances children will be exposed to smoking in movies by age 12. Other images might include photographs of actors who are popular with children smoking in movies rated PG or PG-13 to supplement the photograph of Kate Hudson.

EXERCISE 11.5 Creating a deliberately bad visual argument (p. 227)

Individual response.

EXERCISE 11.6 Revising an ineffective visual argument (p. 227)

Individual response.

PART 3

Grammatical Sentences

12 Understanding Sentence Grammar

EXERCISE 12.1 Identifying subjects and predicates (p. 235)

1. SUBJECT | PREDICATE
   The leaves | fell.
   Sample imitation: The kite soared.
2. SUBJECT | PREDICATE
   October | ends soon.
   Sample imitation: My class begins soon.
3. SUBJECT | PREDICATE
   The orchard owners | made apple cider.
   Sample imitation: The couple grew summer squash.
4. SUBJECT | PREDICATE
   They | examined each apple carefully for quality.
   Sample imitation: They inspected each egg for cracks.
5. SUBJECT | PREDICATE
   Over a hundred people | will buy cider at the roadside stand.
   Sample imitation: Few pool owners will swim at the public beach.

EXERCISE 12.2 Identifying nouns, verbs, and pronouns (p. 235)

1. N V
   The <u>trees</u> <u>died</u>.
2. P V N
   <u>They</u> <u>caught</u> a <u>disease</u>.
3. N V N
   The <u>disease</u> <u>was</u> a <u>fungus</u>.
4. P V N
   <u>It</u> <u>ruined</u> a special <u>grove</u>.
5. P N V N N
   <u>Our</u> <u>great-grandfather</u> <u>planted</u> the <u>grove</u> in the last <u>century</u>.

EXERCISE 12.3 Using nouns and verbs (p. 235)

Possible answers

1. Noun and verb.
   Blow out the candles and make a <u>wish</u>. [Noun.] The child <u>wished</u> for a new bicycle. [Verb.]
2. Noun and verb.
   Many people purchase <u>ties</u> as Father's Day presents. [Noun.] <u>Tie</u> the rope into a square knot. [Verb.]

3. Noun and verb.
   The swing hung from a large oak tree. [Noun.] Ted picked up his niece and swung her around and around. [Verb.]
4. Noun and verb.
   The mail does not come on national holidays. [Noun.] Mail the package to her home address. [Verb.]
5. Verb.
   He spends his free time doing volunteer work.
6. Noun and verb.
   The label bore a poison warning. [Noun.] The companies must label their products. [Verb.]
7. Noun.
   The door flew open by itself.
8. Noun.
   My younger sister was good company.
9. Noun and verb.
   The whistle released us from work. [Noun.] We whistle all the way home. [Verb.]
10. Noun and verb.
    The glue stuck to my hands. [Noun.] We glue our models together. [Verb.]

EXERCISE 12.4 Identifying sentence patterns (p. 239)

1. Find is transitive.
   DO OC
   Many people find New York City exciting.
2. Flock is intransitive.
   No objects or complements.
3. Visit is transitive.
   DO
   Often they visit Times Square first.
4. Are is linking.
   SC
   The Square's lights are astounding.
5. Sell is transitive.
   IO DO
   The flashing signs sell visitors everything from TVs to underwear.

EXERCISE 12.5 Creating sentences (p. 239)

Possible answers

1. The audience laughed.
2. The town elected Flynn mayor.
3. Pip stole the pie.
4. Josie caught the ball.
5. My uncle brought me a cake.
6. Marilou seems unhappy.

7. One candidate called the other a crook.
8. We became reckless.
9. We bought ourselves a television set.
10. No one studied.

EXERCISE 12.6 Identifying and using adjectives and adverbs (p. 241)

ADJ ADJ ADJ
1. The blue water glistened in the hot afternoon sunlight.
   Sample imitation: The blue bird perched on a thin leafy branch.

ADV ADJ
2. Happily, children dipped their toes in the cool lake.
   Sample imitation: Quietly, we peeked into the silent cathedral.

ADV
3. Excitedly, some of the children hopped into the water.
   Sample imitation: Impatiently, two of the children howled for the candy.

ADJ ADV
4. Cautious parents watched from their shady porches.
   Sample imitation: Ambitious runners train for every marathon.

ADV ADV
5. The children played contentedly until the day finally ended.
   Sample imitation: The babies lay still while the singer quietly crooned.

EXERCISE 12.7 Using verb forms as modifiers (p. 241)

Possible answers

1. Jack woke up craving scrambled eggs.
2. The twitching limb relaxed when the sedative took effect.
3. The treasurer's rambling speech covered more topics than I can remember.
4. The typed manuscript contained many errors.
5. Painted birds decorate the window.
6. He wanted to know the origins of the written word.
7. The man escaped the charging animal.
8. We picked the ripened fruit.
9. All the known facts contradict his theory.
10. Driven people may have hypertension.

EXERCISE 12.8 Sentence combining: Single-word modifiers (p. 241)

Possible answers

1. The turn of the twentieth century ushered in improved technology and new materials.
2. A sturdy steel skeleton made the construction of skyscrapers possible.
3. By 1913 the towering Woolworth Building, with its Gothic ornaments, stood 760 feet (55 stories).
4. At 1450 feet the Sears Tower in Chicago now doubles the relatively puny height of the Woolworth Building.

5. Skyscrapers became practical in 1857 when Elisha Graves Otis built the first safe passenger elevator.

EXERCISE 12.9 Identifying prepositional phrases (p. 244)

On July 3, 1863, at Gettysburg, Pennsylvania, Robert E. Lee gambled unsuccessfully for a Confederate victory in the American Civil War. The battle of Pickett's Charge was one of the most disastrous conflicts of the war. Confederate and Union forces faced each other on parallel ridges separated by almost a mile of open fields. After an artillery bombardment of the Union position, nearly 12,000 Confederate infantry marched toward the Union ridge. The Union guns had been silent but suddenly roared against the approaching Confederates. Within an hour, perhaps half of the Confederate soldiers lay wounded or dead.

(Annotations: "On July 3, 1863" — ADVERB; "at Gettysburg, Pennsylvania" — ADVERB; "for a Confederate victory" — ADVERB; "in the American Civil War" — ADJECTIVE; "of Pickett's Charge" — ADJECTIVE; "of the most disastrous conflicts" — ADJECTIVE; "of the war" — ADJECTIVE; "on parallel ridges" — ADVERB; "by almost a mile" — ADVERB; "of open fields" — ADJECTIVE; "After an artillery bombardment" — ADVERB; "of the Union position" — ADJECTIVE; "toward the Union ridge" — ADVERB; "against the approaching Confederates" — ADVERB; "Within an hour" — ADVERB; "of the Confederate soldiers" — ADJECTIVE)

EXERCISE 12.10 Sentence combining: Prepositional phrases (p. 245)

Possible answers

1. The slow loris of Southeast Asia protects itself well with a poisonous chemical.
2. The loris frightens predators when it exudes this chemical from a gland on its upper arm.
3. Unlike a skunk's spray, the loris's chemical is highly toxic even in small quantities.
4. A tiny dose in the mouth can send a human into shock.
5. Predators probably can sense the toxin at a distance with their nasal organs.

EXERCISE 12.11 Identifying verbals and verbal phrases (p. 248)

1. Written in 1850 by Nathaniel Hawthorne (ADJ), *The Scarlet Letter* tells the story of Hester Prynne.
2. Shunned by the community (ADJ), Hester endures her loneliness.
3. Hester is humble enough to withstand her Puritan neighbors' cutting remarks (ADV).
4. Enduring the cruel treatment (ADJ), the determined (ADJ) young woman refuses to leave her home (N).
5. By living a life of patience and unselfishness (N), Hester eventually becomes the community's angel.

EXERCISE 12.12 Sentence combining: Verbals and verbal phrases (p. 248)

Possible answers

1. Air pollution is a health problem affecting millions of Americans.
2. Polluted mainly by industries and automobiles, the air contains toxic chemicals.
3. Environmentalists pressure politicians to pass stricter laws.
4. Wavering politicians are not necessarily against environmentalism.
5. The problems are too complex to be solved easily.

EXERCISE 12.13 Sentence combining: Absolute phrases (p. 250)

Possible answers

1. Her face beaming, Geraldine Ferraro enjoyed the crowd's cheers after her nomination for Vice President.
2. A vacancy having occurred, Sandra Day O'Connor was appointed the first female Supreme Court justice.
3. Her appointment confirmed, Condoleezza Rice became the first female national security advisor.
4. The midterm elections over, Nancy Pelosi was elected the first female minority leader of the House of Representatives.
5. The election won, Elizabeth Dole was the first woman to become a US senator from North Carolina.

EXERCISE 12.14 Identifying subordinate clauses (p. 253)

1. ADJ
   Scientists who want to catch the slightest signals from space use extremely sensitive receivers.
2. ADV
   Even though they have had to fight for funding, these scientists have persisted in their research.
3. ADJ
   The research is called SETI, which stands for Search for Extraterrestrial Intelligence.
4. N (SUBJECT COMPLEMENT)
   The theory is that intelligent beings in space are trying to get in touch with us.
5. N (DIRECT OBJECT)
   Scientists do not yet know what frequency these beings would use to send signals.

EXERCISE 12.15 Sentence combining: Subordinate clauses (p. 254)

Possible answers

1. Moviegoers expect that movie sequels should be as exciting as the original films.
2. Although a few sequels are good films, most are poor imitations of the originals.
3. Whenever a sequel to a blockbuster film arrives in the theater, crowds quickly line up to see it.

4. Viewers pay to see the same villains and heroes whom they remember fondly.
5. Afterward, viewers often grumble about filmmakers who rehash tired plots and characters.

EXERCISE 12.16 Sentence combining: Appositives (p. 256)

Possible answers

1. Some people, geniuses from birth, perform amazing feats when they are very young.
2. John Stuart Mill, a British philosopher, had written a history of Rome by age seven.
3. Paul Klee and Gustav Mahler, two great artists, began their work at age four.
4. Mahler, a Bohemian composer of intensely emotional works, was also the child of a brutal father.
5. As a child the Swiss painter Paul Klee was frightened by his own drawings of devils.

EXERCISE 12.17 Sentence combining: Compound constructions (p. 260)

Possible answers

1. All too often people assume that old age is not a productive time; however, many people in their nineties have had great achievements.
2. In his nineties the philosopher Bertrand Russell spoke vigorously for both international peace and nuclear disarmament.
3. Grandma Moses did not retire to an easy chair; instead, she began painting at age seventy-six and was still going at one hundred.
4. The British general George Higginson and the British archaeologist Margaret Murray published their memoirs after they were ninety.
5. The architect Frank Lloyd Wright designed his first building at age twenty and his last at age ninety.

EXERCISE 12.18 Forming questions and commands (p. 261)

Possible answers

1. Will the water boil?
   Boil the water, please.
2. Did the music stop?
   Stop the music.
3. Have you set the table?
   Set the table.
4. Have you rolled the dice yet?
   Roll the dice.
5. Who can use the telephone?
   Use the telephone.

EXERCISE 12.19 Rewriting passives and expletives (p. 262)

1. Milo Addica and Will Rokos cowrote the screenplay for *Monster's Ball.*
2. Marc Foster directed the film.
3. Only one performance in the movie received an Academy Award.
4. Halle Berry won the award for best actress.

5. The press congratulated Berry for being the first African American to win the award.

EXERCISE 12.20 Identifying sentence structures (p. 263)

1. *Simple:* [MAIN Joseph Pulitzer endowed the Pulitzer Prizes.]
2. *Simple:* [MAIN Pulitzer, incidentally, was the publisher of the New York newspaper *The World*.]
3. *Complex:* [SUBORDINATE Although the first prizes were for journalism and letters only,] [MAIN Pulitzers are now awarded in music and other areas.]
4. *Compound:* [MAIN For example, Berke Breathed won for his *Bloom County* comic strip], and [MAIN Roger Reynolds won for his musical composition *Whispers Out of Time*.]
5. *Compound-complex:* [SUBORDINATE Although only one prize is usually awarded in each category,] [MAIN in 1989 Taylor Branch's *Parting the Waters* won a history prize,] and [MAIN it shared the honor with James M. McPherson's *Battle Cry of Freedom*.]

EXERCISE 12.21 Sentence combining: Sentence structures (p. 264)

Possible answers

1. Recycling takes time, but it reduces garbage in landfills.
2. After people begin to recycle, they generate much less trash.
3. Although white tissues and paper towels biodegrade more easily than dyed ones, people still buy dyed papers.
4. Aluminum cans bring recyclers good money.
5. Environmentalists hope that more communities will recycle newspaper and glass, but many citizens refuse to participate.

13 Case of Nouns and Pronouns

EXERCISE 13.1 Choosing between subjective and objective pronouns (p. 267)

1. I
2. she, I, we
3. She, I
4. her, me
5. her, me

EXERCISE 13.2 Choosing between subjective and objective pronouns (p. 268)

1. us
2. we
3. him
4. us
5. we, I

EXERCISE 13.3 Choosing between *who* and *whom* (p. 270)

1. who
2. who
3. whoever
4. Who
5. Whom

EXERCISE 13.4 Sentence combining: *Who* versus *whom* (p. 270)

1. Some children who have undetected hearing problems may do poorly in school.
2. They may not hear important instructions and information from teachers who speak softly.
3. Classmates whom the teacher calls on may not be audible.
4. Some hearing-impaired children who get a lot of encouragement at home may work harder to overcome their disability.
5. Some hearing-impaired children may take refuge in fantasy friends whom they can rely on not to criticize or laugh.

EXERCISE 13.5 Revising: Case (p. 271)

Written four thousand years ago, *The Epic of Gilgamesh* tells of the friendship of Gilgamesh and Enkidu. Gilgamesh was a bored king who his people thought was too harsh. Then he met Enkidu, a wild man who had lived with the animals in the mountains. Immediately, he and Gilgamesh wrestled to see who was more powerful. After hours of struggle, Enkidu admitted that Gilgamesh was stronger than he. Now the friends needed adventures worthy of the two strongest men on earth. Gilgamesh said, "Between you and me, mighty deeds will be accomplished, and our fame will be everlasting." Among their acts, Enkidu and he defeated a giant bull, Humbaba, and cut down the bull's cedar forests. Their bringing back cedar logs to Gilgamesh's treeless land won great praise from the people. When Enkidu died, Gilgamesh mourned his death, realizing that no one had been a better friend than he. When Gilgamesh himself died many years later, his people raised a monument praising Enkidu and him for their friendship and their mighty deeds of courage.

14 Verbs

EXERCISE 14.1 Using irregular verbs (p. 277)

1. The world population has grown by two-thirds of a billion people in less than a decade. (Past participle.)
2. Recently it broke the 6 billion mark. (Past tense.)
3. Experts have drawn pictures of a crowded future. (Past participle.)
4. They predict that the world population may have slid up to as much as 10 billion by 2050. (Past participle.)
5. Though the food supply rose in the last decade, the share to each person fell. (Both past tense.)

EXERCISE 14.2 Distinguishing *sit/set, lie/lay, rise/raise* (p. 278)

1. Yesterday afternoon the child lay down for a nap.
2. The child has been raised by her grandparents.
3. Most days her grandfather has sat with her, reading her stories.
4. She has risen at dawn most mornings.
5. Her toys were laid out on the floor.

EXERCISE 14.3 Using *-s* and *-ed* verb endings (p. 280)

A teacher sometimes asks too much of a student. In high school I was once punished for being sick. I had missed some school, and I realized that I would fail a test unless I had a chance to make up the classwork. I discussed the problem with the teacher, but he said I was supposed to make up the work while I was sick. At that I walked out of the class. I received a failing grade then, but it did not change my attitude. Today I still balk when a teacher makes unreasonable demands or expects miracles.

EXERCISE 14.4 Using helping verbs (p. 284)

1. Each year thousands of new readers have been discovering Agatha Christie's mysteries.
2. The books were written by a prim woman who had worked as a nurse during World War I.
3. Christie never expected that her play *The Mousetrap* would be performed for decades.
4. During her life Christie was always complaining about movie versions of her stories.
5. Readers of her stories have been delighted to be baffled by her.

EXERCISE 14.5 Revising: Helping verbs plus main verbs (p. 284)

1. A report from the Bureau of the Census has confirmed a widening gap between rich and poor.
2. As suspected, the percentage of people below the poverty level did increase over the last decade.
3. More than 17 percent of the population is making 5 percent of all the income.
4. About 1 percent of the population will be keeping [*or* will keep] an average of $500,000 apiece after taxes.
5. Sentence correct.

EXERCISE 14.6 Revising: Verbs plus gerunds or infinitives (p. 287)

1. A program called HELP Wanted tries to encourage citizens to take action on behalf of American competitiveness.
2. Officials working on this program hope to improve education for work.
3. American businesses find that their workers need to learn to read.
4. In the next ten years the United States expects to face a shortage of 350,000 scientists.
5. Sentence correct.

EXERCISE 14.7 Revising: Verbs plus particles (p. 288)

1. American movies treat everything from going out with [correct] someone to making up [correct] an ethnic identity, but few people look into their significance.
2. While some viewers stay away from [correct] topical films, others turn up at the theater simply because a movie has sparked debate.
3. Some movies attracted rowdy spectators, and the theaters had to throw them out.
4. Filmmakers have always been eager to point their influence out [correct; *or* point out their influence] to the public.
5. Everyone agrees that filmmakers will keep on creating controversy, if only because it can fill up [correct] theaters.

EXERCISE 14.8 Adjusting tense sequence: Past or past perfect tense (p. 295)

1. Diaries that Adolf Hitler was supposed to have written had surfaced in Germany.
2. Many people believed that the diaries were authentic because a well-known historian had declared them so.
3. However, the historian's evaluation was questioned by other authorities who called the diaries forgeries.
4. They claimed, among other things, that the paper was not old enough to have been used by Hitler.
5. Eventually, the doubters won the debate because they had the best evidence.

EXERCISE 14.9 Revising: Tense sequence with conditional sentences (p. 295)

1. When an athlete turns professional, he or she commits to a grueling regimen of mental and physical training.
2. If athletes were less committed, they would disappoint teammates, fans, and themselves.
3. If professional athletes are very lucky, they may play until age forty.
4. Unless an athlete achieves celebrity status, he or she will have few employment choices after retirement.
5. If professional sports were less risky, athletes would have longer careers and more choices after retirement.

EXERCISE 14.10 Revising: Subjunctive mood (p. 298)

1. If John Hawkins had known of the dangerous side effects of smoking tobacco, would he have introduced the dried plant to England in 1565?
2. Hawkins noted that if a Florida Indian were to travel for several days, he would smoke tobacco to satisfy his hunger and thirst.
3. Early tobacco growers feared that their product would not gain acceptance unless it were perceived as healthful.
4. To prevent fires, in 1646 the General Court of Massachusetts passed a law requiring that colonists smoke tobacco only if they were five miles from any town.

5. To prevent decadence, in 1647 Connecticut passed a law mandating that one's smoking of tobacco be limited to once a day in one's own home.

EXERCISE 14.11 Converting between active and passive voices (p. 300)

1. When engineers built the Eiffel Tower in 1889, the French thought it was ugly.
2. At that time industrial technology was still resisted by many people.
3. This technology was epitomized by the tower's naked steel construction.
4. People expected beautiful ornament to grace fine buildings.
5. Further, people could not even call the tower a building because it had no solid walls.

EXERCISE 14.12 Revising: Verb forms, tense, mood (p. 300)

For centuries the natives of Melanesia, a group of islands lying northeast of Australia, have practiced an unusual religion. It began in the eighteenth century when European explorers first visited the islands. The natives were fascinated by the rich goods or "cargo" possessed by the explorers. They saw the wealth as treasures of the gods, and cargo cults eventually arose among them. Over the centuries some Melanesians turned to Christianity in the belief that the white man's religion would bring them the white man's treasures. During World War II, US soldiers, having arrived by boat and airplane to occupy some of the islands, introduced new and even more wonderful cargo. Even today some leaders of the cargo cults insist that the airplane be worshipped as a vehicle of the Melanesians' future salvation.

15 Agreement

Exercise 15.1 Revising: Subject-verb agreement (p. 308)

1. Weinstein & Associates is a consulting firm that tries to make businesspeople laugh.
2. Statistics from recent research suggest that humor relieves stress.
3. Reduced stress in businesses in turn reduces illness and absenteeism.
4. Reduced stress can also reduce friction within an employee group, which then works more productively.
5. In special conferences held by one consultant, each of the participants practices making the others laugh.
6. One consultant to many companies suggests cultivating office humor with practical jokes such as a rubber fish in the water cooler.

7. When the manager or employees regularly post cartoons on the bulletin board, office spirit usually picks up.
8. Sentence correct.
9. In the face of levity, the former sourpuss becomes one of those who hide bad temper.
10. Every one of the consultants cautions, however, that humor has no place in life-affecting corporate situations such as employee layoffs.

EXERCISE 15.2 Revising: Pronoun-antecedent agreement (p. 313)

1. Each girl raised in a Mexican American family in the Rio Grande Valley of Texas hopes that one day she will be given a *quinceañera* party for her fifteenth birthday.
2. Such a celebration is very expensive because it entails a religious service followed by a huge party. *Or:* Such celebrations are very expensive because they entail a religious service followed by a huge party.
3. A girl's immediate family, unless it is wealthy, cannot afford the party by itself.
4. Her parents will ask each close friend or relative if he or she can help with the preparations. *Or:* Her parents will ask close friends or relatives if they can help with the preparations.
5. Sentence correct.

EXERCISE 15.3 Adjusting for agreement (p. 314)

1. Giant pandas are endangered.
2. Conservationists estimate that fewer than two thousand giant pandas live in central China, their natural habitat, because the bamboo forests there are shrinking.
3. Giant pandas eat bamboo and gain most of their nutrition from its leaves and stalks.
4. At the Wolong Wildlife Refuge in China, researchers breed pandas in captivity and release the cubs into the wild when they are old enough to survive on their own.
5. Zoos in the United States wish to raise awareness of the giant panda's plight by breeding pairs of adults and allowing the public to view the adorable cubs while they are young.

EXERCISE 15.4 Revising: Agreement (p. 314)

The writers Richard Rodriguez and Maxine Hong Kingston, despite their differences, share one characteristic: their parents were immigrants to California. A frequent theme of their writings is the difficulties of growing up with two languages and two cultures.

A child whose first language is not English is often ridiculed because he or she cannot communicate "properly." [*Or:* Children whose first language is not English are often ridiculed because they cannot communicate "properly."] Rodriguez learned Spanish at home, but at school classmates and teachers expected him to use their language,

English. He remembers his childish embarrassment because of his parents' poor English. College and graduate school, which usually expand one's knowledge, widened the gap between Rodriguez and his Latino culture. His essays suggest that he lost a part of himself, a loss that continues to bother him.

Kingston spoke Chinese at home and also learned her first English at school. She sometimes writes of these experiences, but more often she writes to recover and preserve her Chinese culture. *The Woman Warrior,* which offers a blend of autobiography, family history, and mythic tales, describes the struggle of Kingston's female relatives. *China Men* focuses on Kingston's male ancestors; each one traveled to Hawaii or California to make money for his wife back in China. Kingston's work, like Rodriguez's essays, reflects the tension and confusion that the child of immigrants often feels when he or she tries [*or:* that the children of immigrants often feel when they try] to blend two cultures.

16 Adjectives and Adverbs

EXERCISE 16.1 Revising: Adjectives and adverbs (p. 318)

1. King George III of England declared Samuel Johnson suitable for a pension.
2. Johnson was taken seriously as a critic and dictionary maker.
3. Thinking about his meeting with the king, Johnson felt proud.
4. Sentence correct.
5. After living cheaply for over twenty years, Johnson finally had enough money from the pension to eat and dress well.

EXERCISE 16.2 Revising: Comparatives and superlatives (p. 320)

Possible answers

1. Charlotte was the oldest of the three Brontë sisters, all of whom were novelists.
2. Some readers think Emily Brontë's *Wuthering Heights* is the saddest novel they have ever read.
3. Sentence correct.
4. Critics still argue about whether Charlotte or Emily wrote better.
5. Certainly, this family of women novelists was unique.

EXERCISE 16.3 Revising: Double negatives (p. 320)

Interest in books about the founding of the United States seems to vary with the national mood. Americans show hardly any interest [or little interest] in books about the founders when things are going well in the United States. However, when Americans can barely [or cannot] agree on major issues, sales of books about the Revolutionary War era increase. During such periods, one cannot go to a bookstore without seeing several new volumes about John Adams, Thomas Jefferson, and other founders. When

Americans feel they have nothing [or don't have anything] in common, their increased interest in the early leaders may reflect a desire for unity.

EXERCISE 16.4 Revising: Present and past participles (p. 322)

1. Several critics found Alice Walker's *The Color Purple* to be a fascinating book.
2. Sentence correct.
3. Another critic argued that although the book contained many depressing episodes, the overall impact was exciting.
4. Since other readers found the book annoying, this critic pointed out its many surprising qualities.
5. In the end most critics agreed that the book was a satisfying novel.

EXERCISE 16.5 Revising: Articles (p. 326)

From the native American Indians who migrated from Asia 20,000 years ago to the new arrivals who now come by planes, the United States is a nation of foreigners. It is a country of immigrants who are all living under a single flag.

Back in the seventeenth and eighteenth centuries, at least 75 percent of the population came from England. However, between 1820 and 1975 more than 38 million immigrants came to this country from elsewhere in Europe. Many children of the immigrants were self-conscious and denied their heritage; many even refused to learn the native language of their parents and grandparents. They tried to "Americanize" themselves. The so-called Melting Pot theory of social change stressed the importance of blending everyone together into a kind of stew. Each nationality would contribute its own flavor, but the final stew would be something called "American."

This Melting Pot theory was never completely successful. In the last half of the twentieth century, an ethnic revival changed the metaphor. Many people now see American society as a mosaic. Americans are once again proud of their heritage, and ethnic differences make the mosaic colorful and interesting.

EXERCISE 16.6 Revising: Adjectives and adverbs (p. 327)

Americans often argue about which professional sport is best: basketball, football, or baseball. Basketball fans contend that their sport offers more action because the players are constantly running and shooting. Because it is played indoors in relatively small arenas, basketball allows fans to be closer to the action than the other sports do. Fans point to how gracefully the players fly through the air to the hoop. Football fanatics say they hardly stop yelling once the game begins. They cheer when their team executes a really complicated play well. They roar more loudly when the defense stops the opponents in a goal-line stand. They yell most loudly when a fullback crashes in for a score. In contrast, the supporters of baseball believe that it might be the perfect sport. It combines the one-on-one duel of pitcher and batter struggling valiantly with the tight teamwork of double and triple plays. Because the game is played slowly and carefully, fans can analyze and discuss the manager's strategy. Besides, they never know when they might catch a foul ball as a souvenir. However, no matter what the sport, all fans feel happy only when their team wins.

EXERCISE ON CHAPTERS 13–16 Revising: Grammatical sentences (p. 327)

Occasionally, musicians become "crossover artists" who can perform well in more than one field of music. For example, Wynton and Branford Marsalis were trained in jazz by their father, the great pianist Ellis Marsalis. Both of the sons have become successful classical artists. Branford's saxophone captures the richness of pieces by Ravel and Stravinsky. Wynton's albums of classical trumpet music from the Baroque period have brought him many awards. Still, if he were to choose which kind of music he likes better, Wynton would probably choose jazz. In contrast to the Marsalises, violinist Nigel Kennedy grew up studying and performing classical music. In his teens he began playing jazz and even rock music. Today he is known almost as well for his interpretations of Miles Davis and Jimi Hendrix as he is for his classical performances.

Such crossovers are often harder for vocalists. Each type of music has its own style and feel that are hard to learn. For example, Kiri te Kanawa, one of the great opera sopranos, has sung popular music and folk songs in concerts and on albums. On each occasion, her technique was nearly perfect, yet she sounded as if she were simply trying to sing properly. It is even more difficult for pop or country vocalists to sing opera, as Linda Ronstadt and Gary Morris found when they appeared in *La Bohème*. Each of them has a clear, pure voice, but a few critics said that he and she lacked the vocal power necessary for opera. However, Bobby McFerrin has been successful singing both pop and classical pieces. He won pop Grammy awards, but he is equally able to sing classical pieces *a cappella* (without musical accompaniment). His voice's remarkable range and clarity allow him to imitate many musical instruments.

No matter how successful, all of these musicians have shown great courage by performing in a new field. They are willing to test and stretch their talents, and each of us music fans benefits.

PART 4

Clear Sentences

17 Sentence Fragments

Exercise 17.1 Identifying and revising sentence fragments (p. 334)

Possible answers

1. Lacks a subject and a verb.
   Complete: An article about vandalism against works of art was interesting.
   Combined: In an interesting article about vandalism against works of art, the author says the vandals' motives vary widely.
2. Lacks a verb.
   Complete: The motives of the vandals vary widely.
   Combined: The motives of the vandals varying widely, researchers can make few generalizations.
3. Complete sentence.
4. Lacks a subject and a verb.
   Complete: But the vandal is not necessarily angry at the artist or the owner.
   Combined: Whoever harms artwork is usually angry, but not necessarily at the artist or the owner.
5. Lacks a verb for the subject man.
   Complete: For instance, a man hammered at Michelangelo's *Pietà*.
   Combined: For instance, a man who hammered at Michelangelo's *Pietà* was angry at the Roman Catholic Church.
6. Lacks a subject.
   Complete: And he knocked off the Virgin Mary's nose.
   Combined: A man hammered at Michelangelo's *Pietà* and knocked off the Virgin Mary's nose.
7. Begins with a subordinating conjunction.
   Complete: He was angry at the Roman Catholic Church.
   Combined: A man hammered at Michelangelo's *Pietà* because he was angry at the Roman Catholic Church.
8. Begins with *which* but is not a question.
   Complete: The Church knew nothing of his grievance.
   Combined: He was angry at the Roman Catholic Church, which knew nothing of his grievance.
9. Begins with a subordinating conjunction.
   Complete: Many damaged works can be repaired.

Combined: Although many damaged works can be repaired, even the most skillful repairs are forever visible.

10. Complete sentence.

Exercise 17.2 Revising: Sentence fragments (p. 336)

1. Human beings who perfume themselves are not much different from other animals.
2. Animals as varied as insects and dogs release *pheromones,* chemicals that signal other animals.
3. Human beings have a diminished sense of smell and do not consciously detect most of their own species' pheromones.
4. The human substitute for pheromones may be perfumes, especially musk and other fragrances derived from animal oils.
5. Some sources say that humans began using perfume to cover up the smell of burning flesh during sacrifices to the gods.
6. No sentence fragment.
7. The earliest historical documents from the Middle East record the use of fragrances, not only in religious ceremonies but on the body.
8. In the nineteenth century chemists began synthesizing perfume oils, which previously could be made only from natural sources.
9. The most popular animal oil for perfume today is musk, although some people dislike its heavy, sweet odor.
10. Synthetic musk oil would help conserve a certain species of deer whose gland is the source of musk.

Exercise 17.3 Revising: Sentence fragments (p. 337)

Possible revision

Baby red-eared slider turtles are brightly colored. Bold patterns on their yellowish undershells serve as a warning to predators. The bright colors of skunks and other animals signal that the animals will spray nasty chemicals. In contrast, the turtle's colors warn largemouth bass that the baby turtle will actively defend itself. When a bass gulps down a turtle, the feisty baby claws and bites, forcing the bass to spit it out. To avoid a similar painful experience, the bass will avoid other baby red-eared slider turtles. The turtle loses its bright colors as it grows too big for a bass's afternoon snack.

18 Comma Splices and Fused Sentences

EXERCISE 18.1 Identifying and revising comma splices (p. 343)

Possible answers

1. Money has a long history. It goes back at least as far as the earliest records.

   Money has a long history that goes back at least as far as the earliest records.

2. Many of the earliest records concern financial transactions; indeed, early history must often be inferred from commercial activity.

   Many of the earliest records concern financial transactions. Indeed, early history must often be inferred from commercial activity.

3. No comma splice.

4. Sometimes the objects have had real value. In modern times, however, their value has been more abstract.

   Sometimes the objects have had real value; in modern times, however, their value has been more abstract.

5. Cattle, fermented beverages, and rare shells have served as money, and each one had actual value for the society.

   Cattle, fermented beverages, and rare shells have served as money. Each one had actual value for the society.

EXERCISE 18.2 Identifying and revising fused sentences (p. 344)

1. Throughout history money and religion were closely linked because there was little distinction between government and religion.

   Throughout history money and religion were closely linked, for there was little distinction between government and religion.

2. The head of state and the religious leader were often the same person. All power rested in one ruler.

   The head of state and the religious leader were often the same person; all power rested in one ruler.

3. These powerful leaders decided what objects would serve as money, and their backing encouraged public faith in the money.

   These powerful leaders decided what objects would serve as money. Their backing encouraged public faith in the money.

4. When coins were minted of precious metals, the religious overtones of money were strengthened.

   Coins were minted of precious metals. The religious overtones of money were then strengthened.

5. People already believed the precious metals to be divine, so their use in money intensified its allure.

   People already believed the precious metals to be divine; their use in money intensified its allure.

EXERCISE 18.3 Sentence combining to avoid comma splices and fused sentences (p. 344)

1. The exact origin of paper money is unknown because it has not survived as coins, shells, and other durable objects have.

2. Perhaps goldsmiths were also bankers; thus they held the gold of their wealthy customers.

3. The goldsmiths probably gave customers receipts for their gold, and these receipts were then used in trade.
4. The goldsmiths were something like modern-day bankers; their receipts were something like modern-day money.
5. The goldsmiths became even more like modern-day bankers when they began issuing receipts for more gold than they actually held in their vaults.

EXERCISE 18.4 Revising: Comma splices and fused sentences (p. 345)

All those parents who urged their children to eat broccoli were right; the vegetable really is healthful. Broccoli contains sulforaphane; moreover, this mustard oil can be found in kale and Brussels sprouts. Sulforaphane causes the body to make an enzyme that attacks carcinogens, substances that cause cancer. The enzyme speeds up the work of the kidneys so that they can flush harmful chemicals out of the body. Other vegetables have similar benefits; however, green, leafy vegetables like broccoli are the most efficient. Thus wise people will eat their broccoli; it could save their lives.

19 Pronoun Reference

EXERCISE 19.1 Revising: Ambiguous and remote pronoun reference (p. 348)

Possible answers

1. There is a difference between the heroes of the twentieth century and the heroes of earlier times: twentieth-century heroes have flaws in their characters.
2. Sports fans still admire Pete Rose, Babe Ruth, and Joe Namath even though none of these heroes could be perfect.
3. Fans liked Rose for having his young son serve as batboy when Rose was in Cincinnati.
4. Rose's reputation as a gambler and tax evader may overshadow his reputation as a ballplayer, but the latter will survive.
5. Rose amassed an unequaled record as a hitter, using his bat to do things no one else has ever done. The record stands even though Rose has been banned from baseball.

EXERCISE 19.2 Revising: Indefinite and inappropriate pronoun reference (p. 351)

Possible answers

1. "Life begins at forty" is a cliché many people live by, and this saying may well be true.
2. When Pearl Buck was forty, her novel *The Good Earth* won the Pulitzer Prize.
3. Buck was a novelist who wrote primarily about China.

4. In *The Good Earth* the characters have to struggle, but fortitude is rewarded.
5. Buck received much critical praise and earned over $7 million, but she was very modest about her success [*or* the praise *or* the money].
6. Kenneth Kaunda was elected to the presidency of Zambia in 1964, at age forty.
7. When Catherine I became empress of Russia at age forty, the Russians feared more than loved her.
8. At forty, Paul Revere made his famous ride to warn American revolutionary leaders that the British were going to arrest them. His warning gave the colonists time to prepare for battle.
9. The members of the British House of Commons did not welcome forty-year-old Nancy Astor as the first female member when she entered in 1919.
10. In AD 610, Muhammad, age forty, began to have a series of visions that became the foundation of the Muslim faith. Since then, millions of people have become Muslims.

EXERCISE 19.3 Revising: Pronoun reference (p. 352)

Possible revision

In Charlotte Brontë's *Jane Eyre,* Jane is a shy young woman who takes a job as governess. Her employer is a rude, brooding man named Rochester. He lives in a mysterious mansion on the English moors, and both the mansion and the moors contribute an eerie quality to Jane's experience. Eerier still are the fires, strange noises, and other unexplained happenings in the house; but Rochester refuses to discuss them. Eventually, Jane and Rochester fall in love. On the day they are to be married, however, Jane learns that Rochester has a wife hidden in the house. The wife is hopelessly insane and violent and must be guarded at all times, circumstances that explain Rochester's strange behavior. Heartbroken, Jane leaves the moors, and many years pass before she and Rochester are reunited.

20 Shifts

EXERCISE 20.1 Revising: Shifts in person and number (p. 354)

1. When a taxpayer is waiting to receive a tax refund from the Internal Revenue Service, he or she begins to notice what time the mail carrier arrives. *Or:* When taxpayers are waiting to receive tax refunds . . . , they begin to notice what time the mail carrier arrives.
2. If the taxpayer does not receive a refund check within six weeks of filing a return, he or she may not have followed the rules of the IRS. *Or:* If taxpayers do not receive refund checks within six weeks of filing a return, they may not have followed the rules of the IRS.

3. If taxpayers do not include their Social Security numbers on returns, they will have to wait for refunds. *Or:* A taxpayer who does not include a Social Security number on a return will have to wait for a refund.
4. When taxpayers do not file their returns early, they will not get refunds quickly.
5. If taxpayers make errors on the tax forms, they might even be audited, thereby delaying refunds even longer. *Or:* If one has made errors on the tax form, he or she might even be audited, thereby delaying a refund even longer.

EXERCISE 20.2 Revising: Shifts in tense and mood (p. 356)

1. When your cholesterol count is too high, adjusting your diet and exercise level reduces it.
2. After you lower your cholesterol rate, you decrease the chances of heart attack and stroke.
3. First eliminate saturated fats from your diet; then consume more whole grains and raw vegetables.
4. To avoid saturated fats, substitute turkey and chicken for beef, and use cholesterol-free salad dressing and cooking oil.
5. A regular program of aerobic exercise, such as walking or swimming, improves your cholesterol rate and makes you feel much healthier.

EXERCISE 20.3 Revising: Shifts in subject and voice (p. 356)

1. If students learn how to study efficiently, they will make much better grades on tests.
2. Conscientious students begin to prepare for tests immediately after they attend the first class.
3. Before each class the students complete all reading assignments, outline the material, and answer any study questions.
4. In class they listen carefully and take good notes.
5. The students ask questions when they do not understand the professor.

EXERCISE 20.4 Revising: Shifts in direct and indirect quotations and questions (p. 358)

1. *Direct:* One anthropologist says, "The functions of marriage have changed, nowhere more dramatically than in industrialized cultures."
   Indirect: One anthropologist says that the functions of marriage have changed, most dramatically in industrialized cultures.
2. *Direct:* May siblings marry? Would the union be immoral?
   Indirect: The question even arises of whether siblings may marry and whether the union would be immoral.
3. *Direct:* The author points out, "Sibling marriage is still illegal everywhere in the United States, and people are still prosecuted under the law."
   Indirect: The author points out that sibling marriage is still illegal everywhere in the United States and that people are still prosecuted under the law.

4. *Direct:* She says, "Incest could be considered a universal taboo. The questions asked about the taboo vary widely."
   Indirect: She says that incest could be considered a universal taboo and that the questions asked about the taboo vary widely.
5. *Direct:* Is the taboo a way of protecting the family? Might it be instinctive?
   Indirect: Some ask whether the taboo is a way of protecting the family or whether it may be instinctive.

EXERCISE 20.5 Revising: Shifts (p. 258)

Possible revision

Driving in snow need not be dangerous if you practice a few simple rules. First, avoid fast starts, which prevent the wheels from gaining traction and may result in the car's getting stuck. Second, drive more slowly than usual, and pay attention to the feel of the car: if the steering seems unusually loose or the wheels do not seem to be grabbing the road, slow down. Third, avoid fast stops, which lead to skids. Be alert for other cars and intersections that may necessitate applying the brakes suddenly. If you need to slow down, reduce the car's momentum by downshifting as well as by applying the brakes. When braking, press the pedal to the floor only if you have antilock brakes; otherwise, pump the pedal in short bursts. If you feel the car skidding, release the brakes, turn the wheel into the direction of the skid, and then press or pump the brakes again. Repeating these motions will stop the skid and reduce the speed of the car.

21 Misplaced and Dangling Modifiers

EXERCISE 21.1 Revising: Misplaced phrases and clauses (p. 360)

1. Women have contributed much of great value to knowledge and culture.
2. In 1821 Emma Willard founded the Troy Female Seminary, the first institution to provide a college-level education for women.
3. Sixteen years later Mary Lyon founded Mount Holyoke Female Seminary, the first true women's college with a campus and directors who would sustain the college even after Lyon's death.
4. *Una,* which was founded by Pauline Wright Davis in 1853, was the first US newspaper that was dedicated to gaining women's rights.
5. Mitchell's Comet, which was named for Maria Mitchell, was discovered in 1847.

EXERCISE 21.2 Using limiting modifiers (p. 361)

Possible answers

1. Almost everybody hates him.
   Everybody almost hates him.
2. Even now I remember the details of the event.
   Now I remember even the details of the event.

3. We hardly heard him call our names.
   We heard him hardly call our names.
4. Write simply.
   Simply write.
5. I nearly missed the performance that was booed off the stage.
   I missed the performance that was nearly booed off the stage.

EXERCISE 21.3 Revising: Squinting modifiers (p. 362)

1. People who often sunbathe can damage their skin. *Or:* People who sunbathe can often damage their skin.
2. Sunbathers who frequently apply a sunscreen block some of the sun's harmful rays. *Or:* Frequently, sunbathers who apply a sunscreen block some of the sun's harmful rays.
3. Men and women who often lie out in the sun have leathery, dry skin. *Or:* Often men and women who lie out in the sun have leathery, dry skin.
4. Doctors tell sunbathers they risk skin cancer when they are older. *Or:* Doctors tell older sunbathers they risk skin cancer.
5. People who usually stay out of the sun will have better skin and fewer chances of skin cancer. *Or:* People who stay out of the sun will usually have better skin and fewer chances of skin cancer.

EXERCISE 21.4 Revising: Separated sentence parts (p. 363)

1. In 1868 Myra Bradwell founded the *Chicago Legal News*.
2. Although she had qualified, Bradwell was later denied admission to the Illinois Bar Association.
3. In an attempt finally to gain admission to the bar, she carried the case to the Supreme Court, but the justices decided against her.
4. Bradwell was determined that no other woman would be denied entrance to a profession if she were qualified.
5. In response to Bradwell's persuasion, the Illinois legislature finally passed a bill ensuring that no one would be restricted from a profession on the basis of gender.

EXERCISE 21.5 Revising: Placement of adverbs and adjectives (p. 365)

1. Some years ago Detroit cars were often praised.
2. Large luxury cars were especially prized.
3. Sentence correct.
4. When ample gasoline supplies returned, consumers again bought large American cars and trucks.
5. Consumers were not loyal to the big vehicles when gas prices rose dramatically.

EXERCISE 21.6 Revising: Dangling modifiers (p. 367)

Possible answers

1. After Andrew Jackson had accomplished many deeds of valor, his fame led to his election to the presidency in 1828 and 1832.
2. By the time Jackson was fourteen, both of his parents had died.

3. To aid the American Revolution, Jackson chose service as a mounted courier.
4. Though not well educated, Jackson proved his ability in a successful career as a lawyer and judge.
5. Because Jackson won many military battles, the American public believed in his leadership.

EXERCISE 21.7 Sentence combining: Placing modifiers (p. 368)

Possible answers

1. As evening falls in the Central American rain forests, the tungara frogs begin their croaking chorus.
2. Croaking loudly at night, male tungara frogs sing "songs" designed to attract female frogs.
3. But predators, also hearing the croaking, gather to feast on the frogs.
4. Lured by their croaking dinners, the predators include bullfrogs, snakes, bats, and opossums.
5. Although the frogs hope to mate, their nightly chorus can result in death instead.

EXERCISE 21.8 Revising: Misplaced and dangling modifiers (p. 368)

Possible revision

Several nights a week, Central American tungara frogs silence their mating croaks. When not croaking, they reduce the chance that they will be eaten by predators. The frogs seem to believe fully in "safety in numbers." More than likely, they will croak along with a large group rather than by themselves. By forgoing croaking on some nights, the frogs prevent the species from "croaking."

22 Mixed and Incomplete Sentences

EXERCISE 22.1 Revising: Sentences mixed in grammar or meaning (p. 372)

Possible answers

1. A hurricane occurs when the winds in a tropical depression rotate counterclockwise at more than seventy-four miles per hour.
2. Because hurricanes can destroy so many lives and so much property, people fear them.
3. Through high winds, storm surge, floods, and tornadoes, a hurricane can kill thousands of people.
4. Many scientists observe that hurricanes in recent years have become more ferocious and destructive.
5. However, in the last half-century, improved communications systems and weather satellites have made hurricanes less deadly.

EXERCISE 22.2 Revising: Repeated sentence parts (p. 372)

1. Global warming is caused by the gradual erosion of the ozone layer that protects the earth from the sun.

2. Scientists who study this problem say that the primary causes of erosion are the use of fossil fuels and the reduction of forests.
3. Many nonscientists mistakenly believe that aerosol spray cans are the primary cause of erosion.
4. One scientist whom others respect argues that Americans have effectively reduced their use of aerosol sprays.
5. He argues that we will stop global warming only when the public learns the real causes.

EXERCISE 22.3 Revising: Incomplete sentences (p. 375)

1. The first ice cream, eaten in China in about 2000 BC, was more lumpy than ice cream in [*or* that in] the modern era.
2. The Chinese made their ice cream of milk, spices, and overcooked rice and packed it in snow to solidify.
3. In the fourteenth century ice milk and fruit ices appeared in Italy and on the tables of the wealthy.
4. At her wedding in 1533 to the King of France, Catherine de Médicis offered more flavors of fruit ices than any other hostess offered.
5. Modern sherbets resemble her ices; modern ice cream resembles her soft dessert of thick, sweetened cream.

EXERCISE 22.4 Revising: Mixed and incomplete sentences (p. 375)

Possible revision

The Hancock Tower in Boston is a thin mirror-glass slab that rises almost eight hundred feet. When it was being constructed, its windows began cracking, and some fell crashing to the ground. In order to minimize risks, the architects and owners replaced over a third of the huge windows with plywood until the problem could be found and solved. With its plywood sheath, the building was homelier than any other skyscraper, the butt of many jokes. Eventually, however, it was discovered that the windows cracked because the joint between the double panes of glass was too rigid. Thicker single-pane windows were installed, and the silly plywood building crystallized into a reflective jewel.

EXERCISE ON CHAPTERS 17–22 Revising: Clear sentences (p. 376)

Possible answers

Many people who are physically challenged have accomplished much, which proves that they are not "handicapped." Confined to wheelchairs, Bob Sampson and Stephen Hawking forged successful careers. Despite his muscular dystrophy, Sampson earned a law degree. He also worked for United Airlines for more than thirty years. Stephen Hawking is most famous for his book *A Brief History of Time*. Hawking is unable to speak, but his voice synthesizer allows him to dictate his books, conduct public lectures, and teach mathematics classes at Cambridge University.

Franklin D. Roosevelt, Ann Adams, and Itzhak Perlman all refused to let polio destroy their lives. Indeed, as President, Roosevelt led the United

States during two of the worst periods of its history: the Great Depression and World War II. Roosevelt inspired hope and determination in the American people, reassuring them with his strong, clear voice. Ann Adams, who was talented in art before polio paralyzed her, knew she had to continue to be an artist. Having retrained herself to draw with a pencil grasped in her teeth, she produced sketches of children and pets. These drawings were turned into greeting cards whose profits sustained her. Roosevelt and Adams were stricken with polio when they were adults; Itzhak Perlman was stricken when he was a child. He was unable to play sports; instead, he studied the violin. Now many think he is greater than any other violinist in the world.

Like Perlman, many physically challenged individuals turn to the arts. Perhaps they do so because [*or:* the reason is that] the joy of artistic achievement compensates for other pleasures they cannot experience. Stevie Wonder, José Feliciano, and Andrea Bocelli all express their souls through their music. Although they are unable to see physically, their music reveals how well they truly see. Hearing impairment struck Ludwig van Beethoven and Marlee Matlin, but it did not stop them from developing their talents. Already a successful composer, Beethoven wrote many of his most powerful pieces after he became deaf. Similarly, Matlin has had excellent acting roles in movies, plays, and television programs; indeed, she won an Oscar for *Children of a Lesser God.* She encourages others to develop their abilities, and she has inspired many hearing-impaired actors.

PART 5

Effective Sentences

23 Emphasizing Ideas

EXERCISE 23.1 Revising: Emphasis of subjects and verbs (p. 380)

Possible answers

1. Many heroes helped to emancipate the slaves.
2. Harriet Tubman, an escaped slave herself, guided hundreds of other slaves to freedom on the Underground Railroad.
3. Tubman risked a return to slavery or possible death.
4. During the Civil War she also carried information from the South to the North.
5. After the war Tubman helped needy former slaves by raising money for refuges.

EXERCISE 23.2 Sentence combining: Beginnings and endings (p. 382)

Possible answers

1. Pat Taylor strode into the packed room, greeting students called "Taylor's Kids" and nodding to their parents and teachers.
2. This wealthy Louisiana oilman had promised his "Kids" free college educations because he was determined to make higher education available to all qualified but disadvantaged students.
3. The students welcomed Taylor, their voices singing "You Are the Wind Beneath My Wings," their faces flashing with self-confidence.
4. They had thought a college education was beyond their dreams, seeming too costly and too demanding.
5. To help ease the costs and demands of getting to college, Taylor created a bold plan of scholarships, tutoring, and counseling.

EXERCISE 23.3 Revising: Series and balanced elements (p. 384)

Possible answers

1. Remembering her days as a "conductor" on the Underground Railroad made Harriet Tubman proud, but remembering her years as a slave made her angry.
2. Tubman wanted freedom regardless of personal danger, whereas her husband, John, wanted personal safety regardless of freedom.

3. Tubman proved her fearlessness in many ways: she disobeyed John's order not to run away, she was a spy for the North during the Civil War, and she led hundreds of other slaves to freedom.
4. To conduct slaves north to freedom, Tubman risked being caught by Southern patrollers, being returned to slavery, and being hanged for a huge reward.
5. After the war Tubman worked tirelessly for civil rights and women's suffrage; she also raised money for homes for needy former slaves.

Exercise 23.4 Emphasizing with repetition or separation (p. 385)

Possible answers

1. One of the few worthwhile habits is daily reading: reading for information, reading for entertainment, reading for a broader view of the world.
2. Reading introduces new words and new styles of expression.
3. Students who read a great deal will more likely write vividly, coherently, and grammatically. They will have learned from other authors.
4. Reading gives knowledge about other cultures, knowledge about history and current events, and knowledge about human nature.
5. As a result of reading, writers have more resources and more flexibility. Thus reading creates better writers.

EXERCISE 23.5 Revising: Conciseness (p. 387)

Possible answers

1. Customers in restaurants must be wary of suggestive selling.
2. In suggestive selling, the waiter asks diners to buy menu selections besides what they ordered.
3. For each item on the menu, another food will naturally complement it.
4. For example, customers will be asked whether they want french fries with a sandwich or a salad with a steak dinner.
5. Customers who give in to suggestive selling often find that their restaurant meals cost more than they had intended to pay.

EXERCISE 23.6 Revising: Emphasizing ideas (p. 387)

Possible revision

Preparing pasta requires common sense and imagination rather than complicated recipes. The key to success is fresh ingredients for the sauce and perfectly cooked pasta. The sauce may contain just about any fresh fish, meat, cheese, herb, or vegetable. The pasta itself may be dried or fresh, although many experienced cooks find fresh pasta more delicate and flavorful. Dried pasta is fine with zesty sauces; fresh pasta is best with light oil and cream sauces. Dried pasta takes longer to cook than fresh pasta does. The cook should follow the package directions and should test the pasta before the cooking time is up. According to the Italians, who ought to know, the pasta is done when the texture is neither tough nor mushy but *al dente,* or "firm to the bite."

24 Using Coordination and Subordination

EXERCISE 24.1 Sentence combining: Coordination (p. 390)

1. Many chronic misspellers do not have the time or the motivation to master spelling rules. They may rely on dictionaries to catch misspellings, but most dictionaries list words under their correct spellings. One kind of dictionary is designed for chronic misspellers. It lists each word under its common *mis*spellings and then provides the correct spelling and definition.
2. Henry Hudson was an English explorer, but he captained ships for the Dutch East India Company. On a voyage in 1610 he passed Greenland and sailed into a great bay in today's northern Canada. He thought he and his sailors could winter there, but the cold was terrible and food ran out. The sailors mutinied and cast Hudson and eight others adrift in a small boat. Hudson and his companions perished.

EXERCISE 24.2 Revising: Excessive or faulty coordination (p. 391)

1. Because soldiers admired their commanding officers, they often gave them nicknames containing the word "old," even though not all of the commanders were old.
2. General Thomas "Stonewall" Jackson was also called "Old Jack," although he was not yet forty years old.
3. Another Southern general, whose full name was James Longstreet, was called "Old Pete."
4. The Union General Henry W. Halleck had a reputation as a good military strategist, and he was an expert on the work of a French military authority, Henri Jomini. Therefore, Halleck was called "Old Brains."
5. After General William Henry Harrison won a victory at the Battle of Tippecanoe, he received the nickname "Old Tippecanoe." He used the name in his presidential campaign slogan "Tippecanoe and Tyler, Too." Although he won the election in 1840, he died of pneumonia a month after taking office.

EXERCISE 24.3 Sentence combining: Subordination (p. 395)

Possible answers

1. When the bombardier beetle sees an enemy, it shoots out a jet of chemicals to protect itself.

   Seeing an enemy, the bombardier beetle shoots out a jet of chemicals to protect itself.

2. Consisting of hot and irritating chemicals, the beetle's spray is very potent.

   The beetle's spray of hot and irritating chemicals is very potent.

3. Stored separately in the beetle's body and mixed in the spraying gland, the spray's two chemicals resemble a nerve-gas weapon.

   The spray's two chemicals, which are stored separately in the beetle's body and mixed in the spraying gland, resemble a nerve-gas weapon.

4. Revolving like a turret on a World War II bomber, the tip of the beetle's abdomen sprays the chemicals.

   Spraying the chemicals, the tip of the beetle's abdomen revolves like a turret on a World War II bomber.

5. Although the beetle defeats most of its enemies, it is still eaten by spiders and birds.

   The beetle defeats most of its enemies except spiders and birds.

EXERCISE 24.4 Revising: Subordination (p. 396)

Possible revision

Fewer students today are majoring in the liberal arts—that is, in such subjects as history, English, and the social sciences. Although students think a liberal arts degree will not help them get jobs, they are wrong. They may not get practical, job-related experience from the liberal arts, but they will get a broad education that will never again be available to them. Many employers look for more than a technical, professional education because they think such an education can make an employee's views too narrow. Instead, they want open-minded employees who can think about problems from many angles. Such flexibility—vital to the health of our society—is just what the liberal arts curriculum instills.

EXERCISE 24.5 Revising: Faulty or excessive subordination (p. 396)

Possible answers

1. Genaro González is a successful writer whose stories and novels have been published to critical acclaim.
2. Although he loves to write, he has also earned a doctorate in psychology.
3. His first story, which is titled "Un Hijo del Sol," reflects his consciousness of his Aztec heritage and place in the world.
4. González writes equally well in English and Spanish. He received a large fellowship, enabling him to take a leave of absence from the University of Texas–Pan American, where he teaches psychology. He could write without worrying about an income.
5. González wrote the first version of "Un Hijo del Sol" while he was a sophomore at Pan American. The university is in the Rio Grande valley of southern Texas, which González calls "el Valle" in the story.

Exercise 24.6 Revising: Coordination and subordination (p. 398)

Possible revision

Sir Walter Raleigh personified the Elizabethan Age, the period of Elizabeth I's rule of England, in the last half of the sixteenth century. Raleigh was a courtier, a poet, an explorer, and an entrepreneur. Supposedly, he gained Queen Elizabeth's favor by throwing his cloak beneath her feet at the right moment, just as she was about to step over a puddle. Although there is no evidence for this story, it illustrates Raleigh's dramatic and dynamic personality. His energy drew others to him, and he was one of Elizabeth's favorites. She supported him and dispensed favors to him. However, he lost his queen's goodwill when without her permission he seduced and eventually married one of her maids of honor. After Elizabeth died, her successor, James I, imprisoned Raleigh in the Tower of London on false charges of treason. Raleigh was released after thirteen years but arrested again two years later on the old treason charges. At the age of sixty-six he was beheaded.

25 Using Parallelism

EXERCISE 25.1 Identifying parallel elements (p. 402)

1. The two sets of parallel phrases (*an automatic or an everyday affair; on solemn occasions and for a special treat*) and the parallel main clauses (. . . *has not always been* . . . *has tended to be*) emphasize the differences between then and now.
2. The parallel verbs (*rolled out* . . . *cooked* . . . *tended* . . . *marked*) stress the number and variety of the women's responsibilities.
3. Supporting *pleasantest* is a wealth of detail expressed in five parallel absolute phrases: *exhaustion* . . . *in; the sated mosquitoes* . . . *off; the room* . . . *garments; the vines* . . . *day;* and *the air conditioner* . . . *mosquitoes.* The phrases convey no action, emphasizing the stillness of the scene.
4. The limiting effects of aging are emphasized by the increasingly narrow parallel verbs—*paints, lies, imprisons*—and the parallel objects—*every action, every movement, every thought.*

EXERCISE 25.2 Revising: Parallelism (p. 402)

Possible answers

1. The ancient Greeks celebrated four athletic contests: the Olympic Games at Olympia, the Isthmian Games near Corinth, the Pythian Games at Delphi, and the Nemean Games at Cleonae.
2. Each day of the games consisted of either athletic events or ceremonies and sacrifices to the gods.
3. In the years between the games, competitors were taught wrestling, javelin throwing, and boxing.

4. Competitors ran sprints, participated in spectacular chariot and horse races, and ran long distances while wearing full armor.
5. The purpose of such events was developing physical strength, demonstrating skill and endurance, and sharpening the skills needed for war.
6. Events were held both for men and for boys.
7. At the Olympic Games the spectators cheered their favorites to victory, attended sacrifices to the gods, and feasted on the meat not burned in offerings.
8. The athletes competed less to achieve great wealth than to gain honor for both themselves and their cities.
9. Of course, exceptional athletes received financial support from patrons, poems and statues by admiring artists, and even lavish living quarters from their sponsoring cities.
10. With the medal counts and flag ceremonies, today's Olympians sometimes seem to be proving their countries' superiority more than demonstrating individual talent.

EXERCISE 25.3 Sentence combining: Parallelism (p. 404)

Possible answers

1. People can develop post-traumatic stress disorder (PTSD) after experiencing a dangerous situation and fearing for their survival.
2. The disorder can be triggered by a wide variety of events, such as combat, a natural disaster, or a hostage situation.
3. PTSD can occur immediately after the stressful incident or not until many years later.
4. Sometimes people with PTSD will act irrationally and angrily.
5. Other symptoms include dreaming that one is reliving the experience, hallucinating that one is back in the terrifying place, and imagining that strangers are actually one's former torturers.

EXERCISE 25.4 Revising: Parallelism (p. 404)

Possible revision

The great white shark has an undeserved bad reputation. Many people consider the great white not only swift and powerful but also a cunning and cruel predator on humans. However, scientists claim that the great white attacks humans not by choice but by chance. To a shark, our behavior in the water is similar to that of porpoises, seals, and sea lions—the shark's favorite foods. These sea mammals are both agile enough and fast enough to evade the shark. Thus the shark must attack swiftly and noiselessly to surprise the prey and give it little chance to escape. Humans become the shark's victims not because the shark has any preference for or hatred of humans but because humans can neither outswim nor outmaneuver the shark. If the fish were truly a cruel human-eater, it would prolong the terror of its attacks, perhaps by circling or bumping into its intended victims before attacking them.

26 Achieving Variety

EXERCISE 26.1 Revising: Varied sentence structures (p. 408)

Possible revision

Charlotte Perkins Gilman was a leading intellectual in the women's movement during the first decades of the twentieth century. Her book *Women and Economics* challenged Victorian assumptions about the differences between the sexes and explored the economic roots of women's oppression. Gilman wrote little about gaining the vote for women, the issue that then preoccupied feminists and that historians have since focused their analyses on. As a result, Gilman's contribution to today's women's movement has often been overlooked.

EXERCISE 26.2 Revising: Varied sentence beginnings (p. 410)

Possible answers

1. Some people are champion procrastinators. Consequently, they seldom complete their work on time.
2. If procrastinators fear criticism or rejection, they will delay completing an assignment.
3. Procrastinators often desire to please a boss or a teacher. Yet they fear failure so much that they cannot do the work.
4. Although procrastination seems a hopeless habit, it is conquerable.
5. Helpfully encouraging procrastinators, teachers or employers can give them the confidence to do good work on time.

EXERCISE 26.3 Revising: Varied sentence beginnings (p. 410)

Possible revision

When scientists in Egypt dug up 40-million-year-old fossil bones, they had evidence of primitive whales. Called mesonychids, the whale ancestors were small, furry land mammals with four legs. These limbs were complete with kneecaps, ankles, and little toes. In contrast, gigantic modern whales have tiny hind legs inside their bodies and flippers instead of front legs. But scientists are certain that these two very different creatures share the same family tree.

EXERCISE 26.4 Writing varied sentences (p. 412)

Possible answers

1. How many cars are registered on this campus?
2. Try to find a parking space on this campus any weekday morning after nine o'clock.
3. What an unexpected pleasure to find a parking space within two blocks of the library!
4. Can the frustration caused by the parking problem be healthy for students? They drive round and round the campus, the minutes of

lost study or class time ticking away. Tension builds. As they pass filled row upon filled row in one lot after another, drivers begin to tremble, sweat, and swear. And the anger and panic, instead of abating when finally the car is safely stowed, stays with the students throughout the day.

EXERCISE 26.5 Analyzing variety (p. 412)

Possible answers

The longest sentence is the first one, a cumulative sentence that establishes a story-telling tone. The question that follows focuses the paragaph on the grandmother's purpose. The next longest sentence, 5, details and stresses the grandmother's accomplishments. Several sentences begin with modifiers, thus avoiding the monotony of starting every sentence with *She* and creating a periodic sentence for emphasis (4), clarifying sequence (6), and putting the gandmother's views in the context of her teaching experience (8). The shortest sentence, the last one, emphasizes the grandmother's success as a teacher, and its inverted word order also emphasizes the verb *soar*.

EXERCISE 26.6 Revising: Variety (p. 412)

Possible revision

<u>After being</u> dormant for many years<u>, </u>the Italian volcano Vesuvius exploded on August 24 in the year AD 79. The ash, pumice, and mud from the volcano buried two towns—Herculaneum <u>and</u> the more famous Pompeii—<u>which</u> lay undiscovered <u>until</u> 1709 and 1748, respectively. The excavation of Pompeii was the more systematic<u>,</u> the occasion for initiating modern methods of conservation and restoration. <u>Whereas</u> Herculaneum was simply looted of its most valuable finds <u>and</u> then left to disintegrate<u>,</u> Pompeii appears much as it did during the eruption. A luxurious house opens onto a lush central garden. An election poster decorates a wall. <u>And</u> a dining table is set for breakfast.

EXERCISE ON CHAPTERS 23–26 Revising: Effective sentences (p. 413)

Possible revision

Modern Americans owe many debts to Native Americans, <u>including several pleasures</u>. Native Americans <u>originated</u> two fine junk foods: <u>popcorn and potato chips</u>.

<u>Native Americans introduced</u> popcorn to the European settlers, <u>Massasoit providing</u> popcorn at the first Thanksgiving feast <u>and the Aztecs offering</u> popcorn to the Spanish explorer Hernando Cortés. The Aztecs <u>and natives of the West Indies</u> wore popcorn necklaces. <u>Native Americans popped</u> the corn in three ways. First, they roasted an ear <u>skewered on a stick</u> over fire <u>and ate the corn that fell</u> outside the flames. Second, they scraped the corn off the cob, <u>threw</u> the kernels into <u>a low</u> fire, <u>and ate</u> the

popped kernels that did not fall into the fire. Third and most sophisticated, they heated a shallow pottery vessel containing sand, stirred corn kernels into the hot sand, and ate what popped up to the surface.

A Native American chef named George Crum devised the crunchy potato chip. In 1853 Crum was cooking at Moon Lake Lodge in Saratoga Springs, New York. A customer complained that Crum's french-fried potatoes were too thick. Crum tried a thinner batch, but these were also unsuitable. Frustrated, Crum deliberately made the potatoes so thin and crisp that they could not be cut with a knife and fork. Crum's joke backfired, for the customer raved about the potato chips. Soon these Saratoga Chips appeared on the lodge's menu and throughout New England. Crum later opened his own restaurant, of course offering potato chips.

Now all Americans munch popcorn in movies, crunch potato chips at parties, and gorge on both when alone and bored. They can be grateful to Native Americans for these guilty pleasures.

PART 6

Punctuation

27 End Punctuation

EXERCISE 27.1 Revising: Periods (p. 419)

1. The instructor asked when Plato wrote *The Republic*.
2. Give the date within one century.
3. The exact date is not known, but it is estimated at 370 BCE.
4. Dr. Arn will lecture on Plato at 7:30 p.m.
5. The area of the lecture hall is only 1600 sq. ft.

EXERCISE 27.2 Revising: Question marks (p. 420)

1. In Homer's *Odyssey*, Odysseus took seven years to travel from Troy to Ithaca. Or was it eight years? Or more?
2. Odysseus must have wondered whether he would ever make it home.
3. "What man are you and whence?" asks Odysseus's wife, Penelope.
4. Why does Penelope ask, "Where is your city? Your family?"
5. Penelope does not recognize Odysseus and asks who this stranger is.

EXERCISE 27.3 Revising: Exclamation points (p. 421)

1. As the firefighters moved their equipment into place, the police shouted, "Move back!"
2. A child's cries could be heard from above: "Help me! Help!"
3. When the child was rescued, the crowd called, "Hooray!"
4. The rescue was the most exciting event of the day.
5. Sentence correct.

EXERCISE 27.4 Revising: End punctuation (p. 421)

When visitors first arrive in Hawaii, they often encounter an unexpected language barrier. Standard English is the language of business and government, but many of the people speak Pidgin English. Instead of an excited "Aloha!" the visitors may be greeted with an excited Pidgin "Howzit!" or asked if they know "how fo' find one good hotel." Many Hawaiians question whether Pidgin will hold children back because it prevents communication with the *haoles,* or Caucasians, who run businesses. Yet many others feel that Pidgin is a last defense of ethnic diversity on the islands. To those who want to make standard English the official language of the state, these Hawaiians may respond, "Just 'cause I speak Pidgin no mean I dumb." They may ask, "Why you no listen?" or, in standard English, "Why don't you listen?"

28 The Comma

EXERCISE 28.1 Punctuating linked main clauses (p. 424)

1. Parents once automatically gave their children the father's surname, but some no longer do.
2. Instead, they bestow the mother's name, for they believe that the mother's importance should be recognized.
3. The child's surname may be just the mother's, or it may link the mother's and the father's with a hyphen.
4. Sometimes the first and third children will have the mother's surname, and the second child will have the father's.
5. Occasionally the mother and father combine parts of their names, and a new hybrid surname is born.

EXERCISE 28.2 Sentence combining: Linked main clauses (p. 425)

Possible answers

1. Parents were once legally required to bestow the father's surname on their children, but these laws have been contested in court and found invalid.
2. Parents may now give their children any surname they choose, and the arguments for bestowing the mother's surname are often strong and convincing.
3. Critics sometimes question the effects of unusual surnames on children, or they wonder how confusing or fleeting the new surnames will be.
4. Children with surnames different from their parents' may suffer embarrassment or identity problems, for giving children their father's surname is still very much the norm.
5. Hyphenated names are awkward and difficult to pass on, so some observers think they will die out in the next generation or before.

EXERCISE 28.3 Punctuating introductory elements (p. 426)

1. Sentence correct.
2. Because it is sudden and apparently well coordinated, the movement of flocks and schools has seemed to be directed by a leader.
3. However, new studies have discovered that flocks and schools are leaderless.
4. When each bird or fish senses a predator, it follows individual rules for fleeing.
5. Multiplied over hundreds of individuals, these responses look as if they have been choreographed.

EXERCISE 28.4 Sentence combining: Introductory elements (p. 426)

Possible answers

1. In an effort to explain the mysteries of flocks and schools, scientists have proposed bizarre magnetic fields and telepathy.

2. Since scientists developed computer models, they have abandoned earlier explanations.
3. Starting with each individual, the movement of a flock or school is rapidly and perhaps automatically coordinated among individuals.
4. Observing that human beings seek coherent patterns, one zoologist suggests that investigators saw purpose in the movement of flocks and schools where none existed.
5. To study the movement of flocks or schools, one must abandon a search for purpose or design.

EXERCISE 28.5 Punctuating essential and nonessential elements (p. 431)

1. Italians insist that Marco Polo, the thirteenth-century explorer, did not import pasta from China.
2. Pasta, which consists of flour and water and often egg, existed in Italy long before Marco Polo left for his travels.
3. Sentence correct.
4. Most Italians dispute this account, although their evidence is shaky.
5. Wherever pasta originated, the Italians are now the undisputed masters in making and cooking it.
6. Sentence correct.
7. Most cooks must buy dried pasta, lacking the time to make their own.
8. Sentence correct.
9. Pasta manufacturers choose hard durum wheat because it makes firmer cooked pasta than common wheat does.
10. Pasta made from common wheat tends to get soggy in boiling water.

EXERCISE 28.6 Sentence combining: Essential and nonessential elements (p. 431)

Possible answers

1. American colonists first imported pasta from the English, who discovered it as tourists in Italy.
2. The English returning from their grand tours of Italy were called macaronis because of their fancy airs.
3. A hair style with elaborate curls was also called *macaroni.*
4. The song "Yankee Doodle" refers to this hairdo when it reports that Yankee Doodle "stuck a feather in his cap and called it macaroni."
5. The song, a creation of the English, was actually intended to poke fun at unrefined American colonists.

EXERCISE 28.7 Punctuating absolute phrases and phrases of contrast (p. 432)

1. Prices having risen rapidly, the government debated a price freeze.
2. A price freeze, unlike a rise in interest rates, seemed a sure solution.
3. The President would have to persuade businesses to accept a price freeze, his methods depending on their resistance.
4. No doubt the President, his advisers having urged it, would first try a patriotic appeal.
5. The President, not his advisers, insisted on negotiations with businesses.

EXERCISE 28.8 Punctuating series and coordinate adjectives (p. 434)

1. Shoes with high heels originated to protect feet from the mud, garbage, and animal waste in the streets.
2. Sentence correct.
3. The heels were worn by men and made of colorful silk brocades, soft suedes, or smooth leathers.
4. High-heeled shoes received a boost when the short, powerful King Louis XIV of France began wearing them.
5. Eventually only wealthy, fashionable French women wore high heels.

EXERCISE 28.9 Punctuating dates, addresses, place names, numbers (p. 436)

1. The festival will hold a benefit dinner and performance on March 10, 2009, in Asheville.
2. The organizers hope to raise more than $100,000 from donations and ticket sales.
3. Performers are expected from as far away as Milan, Italy, and Kyoto, Japan.
4. All inquiries sent to Mozart Festival, PO Box 725, Asheville, North Carolina 28803, will receive a quick response.
5. The deadline for ordering tickets by mail is Monday, December 3, 2008.

EXERCISE 28.10 Punctuating quotations (p. 438)

1. Sentence correct.
2. "I think of the open-ended writing process as a voyage in two stages," Elbow says.
3. "The sea voyage is a process of divergence, branching, proliferation, and confusion," Elbow continues; "the coming to land is a process of convergence, pruning, centralizing, and clarifying."
4. "Keep up one session of writing long enough to get loosened up and tired," advises Elbow, "long enough in fact to make a bit of a voyage."
5. "In coming to new land," Elbow says, "you develop a new conception of what you are writing about."

EXERCISE 28.11 Punctuating to prevent misreading (p. 438)

1. Though happy, people still have moments of self-doubt.
2. In research, subjects have reported themselves to be generally happy people.
3. Among those who have, life has included sufferings as well as joys.
4. Of fifty, eight subjects reported bouts of serious depression.
5. For half, the preceding year had included at least one personal crisis.

EXERCISE 28.12 Revising: Needless or misused commas (p. 442)

1. Nearly 32 million US residents speak a first language other than English.
2. After English the languages most commonly spoken in the United States are Spanish, French, and German.

3. Almost 75 percent of the people who speak foreign languages used the words "good" or "very good" when judging their proficiency in English.
4. Sentence correct.
5. The states with the highest proportion of foreign language speakers are New Mexico and California.

EXERCISE 28.13 Revising: Commas (p. 443)

Ellis Island, New York, reopened for business in 1990, but now the customers are tourists, not immigrants. This spot, which lies in New York Harbor, was the first American soil seen or touched by many of the nation's immigrants. Though other places also served as ports of entry for foreigners, none has the symbolic power of Ellis Island. Between its opening in 1892 and its closing in 1954, over 20 million people, about two-thirds of all immigrants, were detained there before taking up their new lives in the United States. Ellis Island processed over 2000 [*or* 2,000] newcomers a day when immigration was at its peak between 1900 and 1920.

As the end of a long voyage and the introduction to the New World, Ellis Island must have left something to be desired. The "huddled masses," as the Statue of Liberty calls them, indeed were huddled. New arrivals were herded about, kept standing in lines for hours or days, yelled at, and abused. Assigned numbers, they submitted their bodies to the pokings and proddings of the silent nurses and doctors who were charged with ferreting out the slightest sign of sickness, disability, or insanity. That test having been passed, the immigrants faced interrogation by an official through an interpreter. Those with names deemed inconveniently long or difficult to pronounce often found themselves permanently labeled with abbreviations of their names or with the names of their hometowns. But millions survived the examination, humiliation, and confusion to take the last short boat ride to New York City. For many of them and especially for their descendants, Ellis Island eventually became, not a nightmare, but the place where life began.

29 The Semicolon

EXERCISE 29.1 Punctuating between main clauses (p. 445)

1. More and more musicians are playing computerized instruments; more and more listeners are worrying about the future of acoustic instruments.
2. The computer is not the first new technology in music; the pipe organ and saxophone were also technological breakthroughs in their day.
3. Musicians have always experimented with new technology; audiences have always resisted the experiments.
4. Most computer musicians are not merely following the latest fad; they are discovering new sounds and new ways to manipulate sound.

5. Few musicians have abandoned acoustic instruments; most value acoustic sounds as much as electronic sounds.

EXERCISE 29.2 Sentence combining: Related main clauses (p. 445)

Possible answers

1. Electronic instruments are prevalent in jazz and rock music; they are less common in classical music.
2. Jazz and rock change rapidly; they nourish experimentation and improvisation.
3. Traditional classical music does not change; its notes and instrumentation were established by a composer writing decades or centuries ago.
4. Contemporary classical music not only can draw on tradition; it also can respond to innovations such as jazz rhythms and electronic sounds.
5. Much contemporary electronic music is more than just jazz, rock, or classical; it is a fusion of all three.

EXERCISE 29.3 Punctuating main clauses related by conjunctive adverbs or transitional expressions (p. 447)

1. Music is a form of communication like language; the basic elements, however, are not letters but notes.
2. Computers can process any information that can be represented numerically; as a result, they can process musical information.
3. A computer's ability to process music depends on what software it can run; it must, moreover, be connected to a system that converts electrical vibration into sound.
4. Computers and their sound systems can produce many different sounds; indeed, the number of possible sounds is infinite.
5. The powerful music computers are very expensive; therefore, they are used only by professional musicians.

EXERCISE 29.4 Sentence combining: Main clauses related by conjunctive adverbs or transitional expressions (p. 447)

1. Most music computers are too expensive for the average consumer; however, digital keyboard instruments can be inexpensive and are widely available.
2. Inside the keyboard is a small computer that controls a sound synthesizer; consequently, the instrument can both process and produce music.
3. The person playing the keyboard presses keys or other controls; immediately, the computer and synthesizer convert these signals into vibrations and sounds.
4. The inexpensive keyboards can perform only a few functions; still, to the novice computer musician the range of drum rhythms and simulated instruments is exciting.
5. Would-be musicians can orchestrate whole songs from just the melody lines; thus [*or* thus,] they need never again play "Chopsticks."

EXERCISE 29.5 Punctuating long main clauses and series items (p. 448)

1. The Indian subcontinent is separated from the rest of the world by clear barriers: the Bay of Bengal and the Arabian Sea to the east and west, respectively; the Indian Ocean to the south; and 1600 miles of mountain ranges to the north.
2. In the north of India are the world's highest mountains, the Himalayas; and farther south are fertile farmlands, unpopulated deserts, and rain forests.
3. India is a nation of ethnic and linguistic diversity, with numerous religions, including Hinduism, Islam, and Christianity; with distinct castes and ethnic groups; and with sixteen languages, including the official Hindi and the "associate official" English.
4. Between the seventeenth and nineteenth centuries, the British colonized most of India, taking control of government, the bureaucracy, and industry; and they assumed a social position above all Indians.
5. During British rule the Indians' own unresolved differences and their frustrations with the British erupted in violent incidents such as the Sepoy Mutiny, which began on February 26, 1857, and lasted two years; the Amritsar Massacre on April 13, 1919; and violence between Hindus and Muslims during World War II that resulted in the separation of Pakistan from India.

EXERCISE 29.6 Revising: Misused or overused semicolons (p. 450)

1. The main religion in India is Hinduism, a way of life as well as a theology and philosophy.
2. Unlike Christianity and Judaism, Hinduism is a polytheistic religion, with deities numbering in the hundreds.
3. *Possible revision:* Unlike many other religions, Hinduism allows its creeds and practices to vary widely from place to place and person to person. Whereas other religions have churches and principal prophets and holy books, Hinduism does not. And whereas other religions center on specially trained priests or other leaders, Hinduism promotes the individual as his or her own priest.
4. In Hindu belief there are four types of people: reflective, emotional, active, and experimental.
5. Each type of person has a different technique for realizing the true, immortal self, which has infinite existence, infinite knowledge, and infinite joy.

EXERCISE 29.7 Revising: Semicolons (p. 451)

The set, sounds, and actors in the movie captured the essence of horror films. The set was ideal: dark, deserted streets; trees dipping their branches over the sidewalks; mist hugging the ground and creeping up to meet the trees; looming shadows of unlighted, turreted houses. The sounds, too, were appropriate; especially terrifying was the hard, hollow sound of footsteps echoing throughout the film. But the best feature of the movie was its actors, all of them tall, pale, and thin to the point of emaciation. With one exception, they were dressed uniformly in gray and had gray hair. The exception was an actress who dressed only in black, as if to set off her pale yellow, nearly white, long hair, the only color in the film. The glinting black eyes of another actor stole almost every scene; indeed, they were the source of all the film's mischief.

30 The Apostrophe

EXERCISE 30.1 Forming possessives (p. 454)

1. In the myths of the ancient Greeks, the goddesses' roles vary widely.
2. Demeter's responsibility is the fruitfulness of the earth.
3. Athena's role is to guard the city of Athens.
4. Artemis's function is to care for wild animals and small children.
5. Athena and Artemis's father, Zeus, is the king of the gods.
6. Even a single goddess's responsibilities are often varied.
7. Over several centuries' time, Athena changes from a mariner's goddess to the patron of crafts.
8. Athena is also concerned with fertility and with children's well-being, since Athens's strength depended on a large and healthy population.
9. Athena often changes into birds' forms.
10. In Homer's *Odyssey* she assumes a sea eagle's form.
11. In ancient Athens the myths of Athena were part of everyone's knowledge and life.
12. A cherished myth tells how Athena fights to retain possession of her people's land when the god Poseidon wants it.
13. Athena's and Poseidon's skills are different, and each promises a special gift to the Athenians.
14. At the contest's conclusion, Poseidon has given water and Athena has given an olive tree, for sustenance.
15. The other gods decide that the Athenians' lives depend more on Athena than on Poseidon.

EXERCISE 30.2 Distinguishing between plurals and possessives (p. 456)

1. Demeter may be the oldest of the Greek gods, older than Zeus.
2. Many prehistoric cultures had earth goddesses like Demeter.
3. In myth she is the earth mother, which means that the responsibility for the fertility of both animals and plants is hers.
4. The goddess's festival came at harvest time, with its celebration of bounty.
5. The people's prayers to Demeter thanked her for grain and other gifts.

EXERCISE 30.3 Forming contractions (p. 457)

Possible answers

1. She'd rather be dancing.
2. He couldn't see her in the crowd.
3. They're at the front door now.

4. He's my brother.
5. We don't like the beach.
6. She'll speak her mind.
7. The recent storm was nearly as bad as the hurricane of '62.
8. Isn't that your cousin?
9. It's a fact.
10. The door won't budge.

EXERCISE 30.4 Revising: Contractions and personal pronouns (p. 457)

1. In Greek myth the goddess Demeter has a special fondness for Eleusis, near Athens, and its people.
2. Sentence correct.
3. Demeter rewards the Eleusians with the secret for making their land fruitful.
4. The Eleusians begin a cult in honor of Demeter, who's worshipped in secret ceremonies.
5. It's unknown what happened in the ceremonies, for no participant ever revealed their [correct] rituals.

EXERCISE 30.5 Revising: Apostrophes (p. 458)

People whose online experiences include blogging, Web cams, and social-networking sites are often used to seeing the details of other people's private lives. Many are also comfortable sharing their own opinions, photographs, and videos with family, friends, and even strangers. However, they need to realize that employers and even the government can see their information, too. Employers commonly put applicants' names through social-networking Web sites such as *MySpace* and *Facebook*. Many large companies read their employees' outbound e-mail. People can take steps to protect their personal information by adjusting the privacy settings on their social-networking pages. They can avoid posting photos of themselves that they wouldn't want an employer to see. They can avoid sending personal e-mail while they're at work. It's the individual's responsibility to keep certain information private.

31 Quotation Marks

EXERCISE 31.1 Using double and single quotation marks (p. 462)

1. "Why," the lecturer asked, "do we say 'Bless you!' or something else when people sneeze but not acknowledge coughs, hiccups, and other eruptions?"
2. Sentence correct.
3. "Sneezes feel more uncontrollable than some other eruptions," she said.
4. "Unlike coughs and hiccups," she explained, "sneezes feel as if they come from inside the head."
5. She concluded, "People thus wish to recognize a sneeze, if only with a 'Gosh.'"

EXERCISE 31.2 Quoting titles (p. 463)

1. In Chapter 8, titled "How to Be Interesting," the author explains the art of conversation.
2. The Beatles' song "Let It Be" reminds Martin of his uncle.
3. The article that appeared in *Mental Health* [correct] was titled "Children of Divorce Ask, 'Why?'"
4. In the encyclopedia the discussion under "Modern Art" fills less than a column.
5. One prizewinning essay, "Cowgirls on Wall Street," first appeared in *Entrepreneur* [correct] magazine.

EXERCISE 31.3 Revising: Quotation marks (p. 466)

1. In the title essay of her book *"The Death of the Moth" and Other Essays*, Virginia Woolf describes the last moments of a "frail and diminutive body." [Italics are correct for book title, but essay title within it is quoted.]
2. An insect's death may seem insignificant, but the moth is, in Woolf's words, "life, a pure bead."
3. The moth's struggle against death, "indifferent, impersonal," is heroic.
4. Where else but in such a bit of life could one see a protest so "superb"?
5. At the end Woolf sees the moth lying "most decently and uncomplainingly composed"; in death it finds dignity.

EXERCISE 31.4 Revising: Quotation marks (p. 466)

In one class we talked about a passage from "I Have a Dream," the speech delivered by Martin Luther King, Jr., on the steps of the Lincoln Memorial on August 28, 1963:

> When the architects of our republic wrote the magnificent words of the Constitution and the Declaration of Independence, they were signing a promissory note to which every American was to fall heir. This note was a promise that all men would be guaranteed the unalienable rights of life, liberty, and the pursuit of happiness.

"What did Dr. King mean by this statement?" the teacher asked. "Perhaps we should define 'promissory note' first." Then she explained that a person who signs such a note agrees to pay a specific sum of money on a particular date or on demand by the holder of the note. One student suggested, "Maybe Dr. King meant that the writers of the Constitution and Declaration promised that all people in America should be equal." "He and over 200,000 people had gathered in Washington, DC," added another student. "Maybe their purpose was to demand payment, to demand those rights for African Americans." The whole discussion was an eye opener for those of us (including me) who had never considered that those documents make promises that we should expect our country to fulfill.

32 Other Punctuation Marks

EXERCISE 32.1 Revising: Colons (p. 469)

1. In remote areas of many developing countries, simple signs mark human habitation: a dirt path, a few huts, smoke from a campfire.
2. In the built-up sections of industrialized countries, nature is all but obliterated by signs of human life, such as houses, factories, skyscrapers, and highways.
3. The spectacle makes many question the words of Ecclesiastes 1.4: "One generation passeth away, and another generation cometh; but the earth abideth forever."
4. Yet many scientists see the future differently: they hold that human beings have all the technology necessary to clean up the earth and restore the cycles of nature.
5. All that is needed is a change in the attitudes of those who use technology.

EXERCISE 32.2 Revising: Dashes (p. 472)

1. The movie-theater business is undergoing dramatic changes—changes that may affect what movies are made and shown.
2. The closing of independent theaters, the control of theaters by fewer and fewer owners, and the increasing ownership of theaters by movie studios and distributors—these changes may reduce the availability of noncommercial films.
3. Yet at the same time the number of movie screens is increasing—primarily in multiscreen complexes—so that smaller films may find more outlets.
4. The number of active movie screens—that is, screens showing films or booked to do so—is higher now than at any time since World War II.
5. The biggest theater complexes seem to be something else as well—art galleries, amusement arcades, restaurants, spectacles.

EXERCISE 32.3 Revising: Parentheses (p. 473)

1. Many of those involved in the movie business agree that multiscreen complexes are good for two reasons: (1) they cut the costs of exhibitors, and (2) they offer more choices to audiences.
2. Those who produce and distribute films (and not just the big studios) argue that the multiscreen theaters give exhibitors too much power.
3. The major studios are buying movie theaters to gain control over important parts of the distribution process (what gets shown and for how much money).
4. For twelve years (1938–50) the federal government forced the studios to sell all their movie theaters.
5. But because they now have more competition (television and DVD players, for instance), the studios are permitted to own theaters.

EXERCISE 32.4 Using ellipsis marks (p. 477)

1. "To be able to read the Bible in the vernacular was a liberating experience. . . ."
2. "To be able to read the Bible in the vernacular . . . freed the reader from hearing only the set passages read in the church and interpreted by the church."
3. "Women in the sixteenth and seventeenth centuries were educated in the home and, in some cases, in boarding schools. . . . A Protestant woman was expected to read the scriptures daily, to meditate on them, and to memorize portions of them."

EXERCISE 32.5 Revising: Colons, dashes, parentheses, brackets, ellipsis marks, slashes (p. 478)

"Let all the learned say what they can, / 'Tis ready money makes the man." These two lines of poetry by the Englishman William Somerville (1645–1742) may apply to a current American economic problem. Non-American investors with "ready money" pour some of it—as much as $1.3 trillion in recent years—into the United States. The investments of foreigners are varied: stocks and bonds, savings deposits, service companies, factories, art works, even the campaigns of political candidates. Proponents of foreign investment argue that it revives industry, strengthens the economy, creates jobs (more than 3 million, they say), and encourages free trade among nations. Opponents discuss the risks of heavy foreign investment: it makes the American economy vulnerable to outsiders, sucks profits from the country, and gives foreigners an influence in governmental decision making. On both sides, it seems, "the learned say . . . / 'Tis ready money makes the man [or country]." The question is, whose money?

EXERCISE ON CHAPTERS 27–32 Revising: Punctuation (p. 479)

Brewed coffee is the most widely consumed beverage in the world. The trade in coffee beans alone amounts to well over $6,000,000,000 a year, and the total volume of beans traded exceeds 4,250,000 tons a year. It's believed that the beverage was introduced into Arabia in the fifteenth century CE [correct; *or* C.E.], probably by Ethiopians. By the middle or late sixteenth century, the Arabs had introduced the beverage to the Europeans, who at first resisted it because of its strong flavor and effect as a mild stimulant. The French, Italians, and other Europeans incorporated coffee into their diets by the seventeenth century; the English, however, preferred tea, which they were then importing from India. Since America was colonized primarily by the English, Americans also preferred tea. Only after the Boston Tea Party (1773) did Americans begin drinking coffee in large quantities. Now, though, the US [correct; *or* U.S.] is one of the top coffee-consuming countries, consumption having been spurred on by familiar advertising claims—"Good till the last drop"; "Rich, hearty aroma"; "Always rich, never bitter"—and by ubiquitous coffee bars.

Produced from the fruit of an evergreen tree, coffee is grown primarily in Latin America, southern Asia, and Africa. Coffee trees require a hot climate, high humidity, rich soil with good drainage, and partial shade; consequently, they thrive on the east or west slopes of tropical volcanic mountains, where the soil is laced with potash and drains easily. The coffee beans—actually seeds—grow inside bright red berries. The berries are picked by hand, and the beans are extracted by machine, leaving a pulpy fruit residue that can be used for fertilizer. The beans are usually roasted in ovens, a chemical process that releases the beans' essential oil (caffeol), which gives coffee its distinctive aroma. Over a hundred different varieties of beans are produced in the world, each with a different flavor attributable to three factors: the species of plant (*Coffea arabica* and *Coffea robusta* are the most common) and the soil and climate where the variety was grown.

PART 7

Mechanics

33 Capitals

EXERCISE 33.1 Revising: Capitals (p. 487)

1. San Antonio, Texas, is a thriving city in the Southwest.
2. The city has always offered much to tourists interested in the roots of Spanish settlement of the New World.
3. The Alamo is one of five Catholic missions built by priests to convert Native Americans and to maintain Spain's claims in the area.
4. But the Alamo is more famous for being the site of an 1836 battle that helped to create the Republic of Texas.
5. Many of the nearby streets, such as Crockett Street, are named for men who gave their lives in that battle.
6. The Hemisfair Plaza and the San Antonio River link new tourist and convention facilities developed during Mayor Cisneros's terms.
7. Restaurants, hotels, and shops line the river. The haunting melodies of "Una Paloma Blanca" and "Malagueña" lure passing tourists into Casa Rio and other excellent Mexican restaurants.
8. The University of Texas at San Antonio has expanded, and a medical center has been developed in the northwest part of the city.
9. Sentence correct.
10. The city has attracted high-tech industry, creating a corridor of economic growth between San Antonio and Austin and contributing to the Texas economy.

34 Italics or Underlining

EXERCISE 34.1 Revising: Italics or underlining (p. 491)

1. Of the many Vietnam veterans who are writers, Oliver Stone is perhaps the most famous for writing and directing the films *Platoon* and *Born on the Fourth of July*.
2. Tim O'Brien has written short stories for *Esquire*, *GQ*, and *Massachusetts Review*.
3. *Going After Cacciato* is O'Brien's dreamlike novel about the horrors of combat.
4. The word *Vietnam* is technically two words (*Viet* and *Nam*), but most American writers spell it as *one* word. [*Viet* and *Nam* were correctly italicized.]

5. American writers use words or phrases borrowed from Vietnamese, such as *di di mau* ("go quickly") or *dinky dau* ("crazy").
6. Philip Caputo's gripping account of his service in Vietnam appears in the book *A Rumor of War*.
7. Sentence correct.
8. David Rabe's plays—including *The Basic Training of Pavlo Hummel*, *Streamers*, and *Sticks and Bones*—depict the effects of the war not only on the soldiers but also on their families.
9. Called "the poet laureate of the Vietnam war," Steve Mason has published two collections of poems: *Johnny's Song* and *Warrior for Peace*.
10. *The Washington Post* published rave reviews of *Veteran's Day*, an autobiography by Rod Kane.

35 Abbreviations

EXERCISE 35.1 Revising: Abbreviations (p. 495)

1. In the September 17, 2003, issue of *Science* magazine, Virgil L. Sharpton discusses a theory that could help explain the extinction of dinosaurs.
2. About 65 million years ago, a comet or asteroid crashed into the earth.
3. The result was a huge crater about 10 kilometers (6.2 miles) deep in the Gulf of Mexico.
4. Sharpton's new measurements suggest that the crater is 50 percent larger than scientists previously believed.
5. Indeed, 20-year-old drilling cores reveal that the crater is about 186 miles wide, roughly the size of Connecticut.
6. Sentence correct.
7. On impact, 200,000 cubic kilometers of rock and soil were vaporized or thrown into the air.
8. That's the equivalent of 2.34 billion cubic feet of matter.
9. The impact would have created 400-foot tidal waves across the Atlantic Ocean, temperatures higher than 20,000 degrees, and powerful earthquakes.
10. Sharpton theorizes that the dust, vapor, and smoke from this impact blocked the sun's rays for months, cooled the earth, and thus resulted in the death of the dinosaurs.

36 Numbers

EXERCISE 36.1 Revising: Numbers (p. 498)

1. The planet Saturn is 900 million miles, or nearly 1.5 billion kilometers, from the sun.
2. Sentence correct.

3. Thus, Saturn orbits the sun only 2.4 times during the average human life span.
4. It travels in its orbit at about 21,600 miles per hour.
5. Fifteen to twenty times denser than Earth's core, Saturn's core measures seventeen thousand miles across.
6. The temperature at Saturn's cloud tops is –170 degrees Fahrenheit.
7. In 1933, astronomers found on Saturn's surface a huge white spot two times the size of Earth and seven times the size of Mercury.
8. Saturn's famous rings reflect almost 70 percent of the sunlight that approaches the planet.
9. The ring system is almost 40,000 miles wide, beginning 8800 miles from the planet's visible surface and ending 47,000 miles from that surface.
10. Saturn generates about 130 trillion kilowatts of electricity.

EXERCISE ON CHAPTERS 33–36 Revising: Mechanics (p. 498)

According to many sources—for example, the *Cambridge Ancient History* and *Gardiner's Egypt of the Pharaohs* [titles italicized]—the ancient Egyptians devoted much attention to making life more convenient and pleasurable for themselves.

Our word *pharaoh* [defined word italicized] for the ancient Egyptian rulers comes from the Egyptian word *pr'o* [foreign word italicized], meaning "great house." Indeed, the Egyptians placed great emphasis on family residences, adding small bedrooms as early as 3500 BCE. By 3000 BCE, the Egyptians made ice through evaporation of water at night and then used it to cool their homes. About the same time they used fans made of palm fronds or papyrus to cool themselves in the day. To light their homes, the Egyptians abandoned the animal-fat lamps humans had used for fifty thousand years. Instead, around 1300 BCE the people of Egypt devised the first oil lamps.

Egyptians found great pleasure in playing games. Around 4300 years ago they created one of the oldest board games known. The game involved racing ivory or stone pieces across a papyrus playing board. By 3000 BCE, Egyptian children played marbles with semiprecious stones, some of which have been found in gravesites at Nagada, Egypt. Around 1360 BCE, small children played with clay rattles covered in silk and shaped like animals.

To play the game of love, Egyptian men and women experimented with cosmetics applied to skin and eyelids. Kohl, history's first eyeliner, was used by both sexes to ward off evil. Five thousand years ago Egyptians wore wigs made of vegetable fibers or human hair. In 900 BCE, Queen Isimkheb wore a wig so heavy that she needed assistance in walking. To adjust their make-up and wigs, Egyptians adapted the simple metal mirrors devised by the Sumerians in the Bronze Age, ornamenting them with carved handles of ivory, gold, or wood. Feeling that only those who smelled sweet could be attractive, the Egyptians made deodorants from perfumed oils, for example, cinnamon and citrus.

PART 8

Effective Words

37 Using Appropriate Language

EXERCISE 37.1 Revising: Appropriate words (p. 510)

1. Acquired immune deficiency syndrome (AIDS) is a serious threat all over the world.
2. The disease is transmitted primarily by sexual intercourse, exchange of bodily fluids, shared needles, and blood transfusions.
3. Those who think the disease is limited to homosexuals, drug users, and foreigners are quite mistaken.
4. Statistics suggest that in the United States one in every five hundred college students carries the virus.
5. People with AIDS do not deserve others' exclusion or callousness. Instead, they need all the compassion, medical care, and financial assistance due the seriously ill.
6. A person with AIDS often sees a team of doctors or a single doctor with a specialized practice.
7. The doctor may help patients by obtaining social services for them as well as providing medical care.
8. The person with AIDS who loses his or her job may need public assistance.
9. For someone who is very ill, a full-time nurse may be necessary. The nurse can administer medications and make the sick person as comfortable as possible.
10. Some people with AIDS have insurance, but others lack the money for premiums.

38 Using Exact Language

EXERCISE 38.1 Using a dictionary (p. 513)

The answers to this exercise will depend on the dictionary being consulted. Each one uses a different notation system, and in some cases they disagree over syllable divisions. Thus, no answers are provided.

EXERCISE 38.2 Revising: Denotation (p. 515)

1. Maxine Hong Kingston was awarded many prizes for her first two books, *The Woman Warrior* and *China Men*.

2. Kingston cites her mother's tales about ancestors and ancient Chinese customs as the sources of these memoirs.
3. In her childhood Kingston was greatly affected by her mother's tale about a pregnant aunt who was ostracized by villagers. [*Ostracized* correct.]
4. The aunt gained vengeance by drowning herself in the village's water supply.
5. Kingston decided to make her nameless relative famous by giving her immortality in *The Woman Warrior.* [*Immortality* correct.]

EXERCISE 38.3 Considering the connotations of words (p. 515)

1. AIDS is a serious health problem.
2. Once the virus has entered the blood system, it destroys T-cells.
3. The function of T-cells is to combat infections.
4. Without enough T-cells, the body is nearly defenseless against infections.
5. To prevent exposure to the disease, one should be especially cautious in sexual relationships.

EXERCISE 38.4 Revising: Concrete and specific words (p. 517)

Possible revision

I remember as if it were last week how frightened I felt the first time I crossed the threshold of Mrs. Murphy's second-grade class. Just three days before, I had moved from a rural one-street town in Missouri to a suburb of Chicago where the houses and the people were jammed together. My new school looked monstrous from the outside and seemed forbiddingly dim inside as I walked haltingly down the endless corridor toward the classroom. The class was clamorous as I neared the door; but when I slipped inside, twenty faces became still and gawked at me. I felt terrified and longed for a place to hide. However, in a booming voice Mrs. Murphy ordered me to the front of the room to introduce myself.

EXERCISE 38.5 Using concrete and specific words (p. 517)

Possible answers

1. fabric, upholstery fabric, velvet
   She chose a wine-colored velvet for backing the pillow.
2. delicious, tart, lemony
   He made a meringue pie, lemony and delicately brown.
3. car, foreign car, Volvo station wagon
   He bought a 1973 Volvo station wagon.
4. narrow-minded, prejudiced, sexist
   My uncle's sexist attitudes cause many arguments in our family.
5. reach, stretch, lunge
   Each child lunged for the prize thrown by the clown.
6. green, dark green, bilious green
   The algae covered the surface with a bilious green scum.

7. walk, march, goose-step
   The soldiers goose-stepped menacingly.
8. flower, daisy, ox-eyed daisy
   Some people call the ox-eyed daisy a "brown-eyed Susan."
9. serious, solemn, grim
   His grim expression frightened us.
10. pretty; with small, regular features; with a button nose and a tiny, smiling mouth
    The infant, with a button nose and a tiny, smiling mouth, was a perfect model for baby products.
11. teacher, history teacher, American history teacher
    My American history teacher requires three research papers.
12. nice, considerate, sympathetic
    I need a sympathetic friend.
13. virtue, honesty, frankness
    His frankness was refreshing after I had heard so much flattery.
14. angry, furious, raging
    Raging uncontrollably, Andy insulted everyone around him.
15. crime, theft, armed robbery
    Drug addicts sometimes commit armed robbery to pay for their habits.

EXERCISE 38.6 Using prepositions in idioms (p. 519)

1. Children are waiting longer to become independent of their parents.
2. According to US Census data for young adults ages eighteen to twenty-four, 57 percent of men and 47 percent of women live full-time with their parents.
3. Some of these adult children are dependent on their parents financially.
4. In other cases, the parents charge their children for housing, food, and other living expenses.
5. Many adult children are financially capable of living independently but prefer to save money rather than contend with high housing costs.

EXERCISE 38.7 Analyzing figurative language (p. 521)

1. *A delta wing out of nightmare* is a metaphor. *Like a stingray crossing upstream* is a simile. Both convey the menace of an airplane and its shadow.
2. *Her roots ran deep into the earth* and *from those roots she drew strength* are both metaphors establishing the person's indomitability.
3. *Outdistanced unpleasant sensations* and *headed for the freedom of open fields* are both metaphors equating Angelou's sense of release with the runner's freedom.
4. *Lash of adverse criticism* is a metaphor that makes clear the power of words to hurt.

5. The judge is like a *chickadee* and the roomful of writers is like a *caucus of crows*—two similes that convey the judge's powerlessness in the face of the writers' bombast.

EXERCISE 38.8 Using figurative language (p. 521)

Individual response.

EXERCISE 38.9 Revising: Trite expressions (p. 523)

Possible answers

1. These disasters of the war have shaken the small nation severely.
2. Prices for food have risen markedly, and citizens suspect that others are profiting on the black market.
3. Medical supplies are so scarce that even very sick civilians cannot get treatment.
4. With most men fighting or injured or killed, women have had to take the men's places in farming and manufacturing.
5. Finally, the war's high cost has destroyed the nation's economy.

39 Writing Concisely

EXERCISE 39.1 Revising: Subjects and verbs; empty words and phrases (p. 526)

Possible answers

1. *Gerrymandering* means redrawing the lines of a voting district to benefit a particular party or ethnic group.
2. The name refers to Elbridge Gerry, who as governor of Massachusetts in 1812 redrew voting districts in Essex County.
3. On the map one new district looked like a salamander.
4. Upon seeing the map, a critic of Governor Gerry's administration cried out, "Gerrymander!"
5. Now a political group may try to change a district's voting pattern by gerrymandering to exclude rival groups' supporters.

EXERCISE 39.2 Revising: Unnecessary repetition (p. 528)

Possible answers

1. After their tours of duty, some Vietnam veterans had problems readjusting to life in America.
2. Afflicted with post-traumatic stress disorder, some veterans had trouble holding jobs and maintaining relationships.
3. Some who used drugs in Vietnam could not break their habits after they returned to the United States.
4. The few veterans who committed crimes and violent acts gained so much notoriety that many Americans thought all veterans were crazy.
5. As a result of such stereotyping, Vietnam-era veterans are protected by antidiscrimination laws.

EXERCISE 39.3 Revising: Conciseness (p. 530)

Possible answers

1. The Mexican general Antonio López de Santa Anna introduced chewing gum to the United States.
2. After his defeat by the Texans in 1845, the exiled general chose to settle in New York.
3. In his baggage the general had stashed a piece of chicle, the dried milky sap of the Mexican sapodilla tree.
4. Santa Anna's friend Thomas Adams brought more of this resin into the country, planning to make rubber.
5. When the plan failed, Adams got a much more successful idea from the way General Santa Anna used the resin, as a gum for chewing.

EXERCISE 39.4 Revising: Conciseness (p. 530)

Possible answers

After much thought, he concluded that carcinogens could be treated like automobiles. Instead of giving in to a fear of cancer, we should balance the benefits we receive from potential carcinogens (such as plastic and pesticides) against the damage they do. Similarly, instead of responding irrationally to the pollution caused by automobiles, we have decided to live with them and enjoy their benefits while simultaneously working to improve them.

40 Spelling and the Hyphen

EXERCISE 40.1 Distinguishing between *ie* and *ei* (p. 535)

1. brief
2. deceive
3. receipt
4. seize
5. foreign
6. priest
7. grievance
8. fiend
9. leisurely
10. achieve
11. patience
12. pierce
13. height
14. freight
15. feint
16. sieve

EXERCISE 40.2 Keeping or dropping a final *e* (p. 536)

1. malicious
2. lovable *or* loveable
3. serviceable
4. retirement
5. suing
6. virtuous
7. notable
8. battling
9. suspension

EXERCISE 40.3 Keeping or dropping a final *y* (p. 536)

1. implies
2. messier
3. applying
4. delaying
5. defiance
6. says
7. solidifies
8. Murphys
9. supplied

EXERCISE 40.4 Doubling consonants (p. 537)

1. repairing
2. admittance
3. benefited
4. shopped
5. concealed
6. allotted
7. dripping
8. declaimed
9. paralleling

EXERCISE 40.5 Forming plurals (p. 538)

1. piles
2. donkeys
3. beaches
4. summaries
5. miles per hour
6. boxes
7. switches
8. sisters-in-law
9. Baleses
10. cupfuls
11. librettos *or* libretti
12. videos
13. thieves
14. geese
15. hisses
16. appendixes *or* appendices

EXERCISE 40.6 Using hyphens in compound words (p. 546)

1. Correct
2. de-escalate
3. forty-odd soldiers
4. little-known bar
5. seven-eighths
6. seventy-eight
7. happy-go-lucky
8. pre-existing
9. senator-elect
10. Correct
11. two- and six-person cars
12. ex-songwriter
13. V-shaped
14. re-educate

PART 9

Research Writing

41 Planning a Research Project

EXERCISE 41.1 Finding a topic and question (p. 553)

Individual response.

EXERCISE 41.2 Developing a research strategy (p. 557)

Individual response.

EXERCISE 41.3 Compiling an annotated working bibliography (p. 561)

Individual response.

42 Finding Sources

EXERCISE 42.1 Using the library (p. 588)

Individual response.

EXERCISE 42.2 Finding library sources (p. 589)

Individual response.

EXERCISE 42.3 Finding Web sources (p. 589)

Individual response.

43 Working with Sources

EXERCISE 43.1 Evaluating a source (p. 603)

Responses will vary. Packard's book is famously critical of advertising methods. Students should recognize Packard's bias while also valuing his expertise and evidence.

EXERCISE 43.2 Evaluating Web sites (p. 603)

Individual response.

EXERCISE 43.3 Evaluating a blog (p. 604)

Individual response.

EXERCISE 43.4 Evaluating an online discussion (p. 604)

Individual response.

EXERCISE 43.5 Synthesizing sources (p. 606)

The key similarities and differences are these:

Similarities: Nadelmann and Posey agree that crackdowns or penalties do not stop the drug trade. Nadelmann and Runkle agree that the drug trade affects the young, who are most impressionable.

Differences: Nadelmann maintains that the illegal drug trade does more to entice youths to drugs than do the drugs themselves, whereas Runkle maintains that the illegality discourages youths from using prohibited drugs. Posey, in contrast to Runkle, claims that penalties do nothing to discourage drug abusers.

Students' paragraphs will depend on their views, but here is a sample response:

Posey seems to invalidate the whole debate over drug legalization: nothing, he says from experience, will stop drug abuse. But such a futile view, whatever its truth, cannot stop the search for a solution. We have tried the prohibition favored by Runkle. Even if, as she claims, students are using fewer illegal drugs, prohibition has not worked. It may be time to try the admittedly risky approach proposed by Nadelmann, legalizing drugs to "drive the drug-dealing business off the streets."

EXERCISE 43.6 Evaluating and synthesizing sources (p. 607)

Individual response.

EXERCISE 43.7 Summarizing and paraphrasing (p. 619)

Possible summary

Eisinger et al. 44

Federalism, unlike a unitary system, allows the states autonomy. Its strength and its weakness—which are in balance—lie in the regional differences it permits.

Possible paraphrase

Eisinger et al. 44

Under federalism, each state can devise its own ways of handling problems and its own laws. The system's advantage is that a state can operate according to its people's culture, morals, and wealth. A unitary system like that in France does not permit such diversity.

EXERCISE 43.8 Combining summary, paraphrase, and direct quotation (p. 619)

Possible summary

Farb 107

Speakers at parties often "unconsciously duel" in conversations in order to assert "dominance" over others. A speaker may mumble, thus preventing a listener from understanding what is said. Or he or she may continue talking after the listener has moved away, a "challenge to the listener to return and acknowledge the dominance of the speaker."

EXERCISE 43.9 Gathering information from sources (p. 620)

Individual response.

EXERCISE 43.10 Introducing and interpreting borrowed material (p. 625)

Sample paragraph

Why does a woman who is otherwise happy regularly suffer anxiety attacks at the first sign of spring? Why does a man who is otherwise a competent, relaxed driver feel panic whenever he approaches a traffic rotary? According to Willard Gaylin, a professor of psychiatry and a practicing psychoanalyst, such feelings of anxiety are attributable to the uniquely human capacities for remembering, imagining, and forming "symbolic and often unconscious representations" of experiences (23). The feeling of anxiety, Gaylin says, "is . . . compounded by its seemingly irrational quality": it may appear despite the absence of an immediate source of worry or pain (23). The anxious woman is not aware of it, but her father's death twenty years before in April has caused her to equate spring with death. Similarly, the man has forgotten that a terrible accident he witnessed as a child occurred at a rotary. For both people, the anxious feelings are not reduced but heightened because they seem to be unfounded.

44 Avoiding Plagiarism and Documenting Sources

EXERCISE 44.1 Recognizing plagiarism (p. 631)

1. Plagiarized: takes phrases directly from the original without quotation marks.
2. Acceptable: acknowledges the source, uses quotation marks around copied words, and uses brackets around an addition to the quotation.
3. Inaccurate and plagiarized: the passage uses phrases from the original without quotation marks and distorts its meaning.
4. Acceptable: acknowledges the source, restates the original in new words, and correctly conveys the original's meaning.
5. Inaccurate and plagiarized: fails to acknowledge the source and fails to convey accurately the concepts of "discrimination" and "confusing" outlined in the original.
6. Inaccurate: ellipses are needed to indicate that material was omitted, and brackets must be placed around lowercase *s* to indicate revision. In addition, the editing of the passage omits mention of "psychiatric labeling," the focus of the original.

45 Writing the Paper

EXERCISE 45.1 Developing a thesis statement (p. 637)

Individual response.

EXERCISE 45.2 Creating a structure (p. 640)

Individual response.

EXERCISE 45.3 Drafting your paper (p. 641)

Individual response.

EXERCISE 45.4 Revising and editing your paper (p. 643)

Individual response.

EXERCISE 45.5 Preparing and proofreading your final draft (p. 643)

Individual response.

46 Using MLA Documentation and Format

EXERCISE 46.1 Writing works-cited entries (p. 688)

The citations below are in MLA style and are alphabetized.

Eggert, Wayne G. "State and Local Sales/Use Tax Simplification." *The Sales Tax in the Twenty-first Century*. Ed. Matthew N. Murray and William F. Fox. Westport: Praeger, 2004. 67-80. Print.

"The Internet Tax Freedom Act and the Digital Divide." *Center on Budget and Policy Priorities*. Center on Budget and Policy Priorities, 26 Sept. 2007. Web. 2 Nov. 2008.

James, Nora. E-mail interview. 1 Nov. 2008.

Novack, Janet. "Point, Click, Pay Tax." *Forbes* 28 Nov. 2007: 56-58. *Proquest*. Web. 10 Nov. 2008.

Osborne, Sally G. *All's Fair in Internet Commerce, or Is It?* New York: Random, 2004. Print.

United States. Advisory Commission on Electronic Commerce. *Report to Congress*. US Advisory Commission on Electronic Commerce, Apr. 2005. Web. 12 Nov. 2008.

Zimmerman, Malai, and Kent Hoover. "Use of Third Parties to Collect State and Local Taxes on Internet Sales." *Pacific Business Journal* 5.2 (2004): 45-48. Print.

47 Two Research Papers in MLA Style

There are no exercises in Chapter 47.

PART 10

Writing in the Academic Disciplines

48 Working with the Goals and Requirements of the Disciplines

Chapter 48 does not have any exercises.

49 Reading and Writing About Literature

Chapter 49 does not have any exercises.

50 Writing in Other Humanites

Chapter 50 does not have any exercises.

51 Writing in the Social Sciences

Chapter 51 does not have any exercises.

52 Writing in the Natural and Applied Sciences

Chapter 52 does not have any exercises.

PART 11

Special Writing Situations

53 Essay Examinations

Chapter 53 does not have any exercises.

54 Writing Online

Chapter 54 does not have any exercises.

55 Public Writing

Chapter 55 does not have any exercises.

56 Oral Presentations

Chapter 56 does not have any exercises.